COLLEGE MATHEMATICS FOR BEGINNERS

The Ultimate Step by Step Guide to Acing College Mathematics

By

Reza Nazari

All inquiries should be addressed to:

info@EffortlessMath.com

www.EffortlessMath.com

ISBN: 978-1-63719-563-5

Published by: **Effortless Math Education Inc.**

For Online Math Practice Visit www.EffortlessMath.com

Welcome to
College Math
2024

Thank you for choosing Effortless Math for your College Math preparation.

Embark on your journey to mathematical mastery with our "College Mathematics for Beginners" guide. By choosing this resource for your college math test preparation, you're taking an important step towards academic success. This guide is designed to be a pivotal tool in achieving the highest score you can attain.

For those who have found math challenging, this book is a beacon of hope. It's structured to help you not just pass, but to excel in your college math assessments. As the exam date approaches, remember that preparation is key. This all-inclusive study companion is here to ensure you're thoroughly prepared for what lies ahead.

Keep in mind that this guide is intended to be a study companion rather than a traditional textbook. Every chapter of this "self-directed math guide" is crafted with the intention of making your study time as productive as possible.
In line with the 2024 curriculum, *College Mathematics for Beginners* aims to sharpen your mathematical skills, reduce test anxiety, and increase your confidence. With this guide, you're not just studying; you're equipping yourself with the tools for success on your college math exams.

How to Use This Book Effectively

Embarking on your journey to conquer the challenges of college mathematics begins with this comprehensive guide. Here, each chapter is a stepping stone towards a deeper understanding and mastery of the concepts you'll encounter in your college math exams.

Success is built on a foundation of thorough understanding, which is why this book emphasizes a methodical approach. Engage with each topic fully before progressing to the next, cementing your knowledge and ensuring your preparedness. The book is structured to offer examples and step-by-step explanations that will demystify complex mathematical concepts.

To get the best possible results from this book:

➢ **Begin studying long before your test date**. This provides you ample time to learn the different math concepts. The earlier you begin studying for the test, the sharper your skills will be. Do not procrastinate! Provide yourself with plenty of time to learn the concepts and feel comfortable that you understand them when your test date arrives.

➢ **Practice consistently**. Study Math concepts at least 20 to 30 minutes a day. Remember, slow and steady wins the race, which can be applied to preparing for the College Math test. Instead of cramming to tackle everything at once, be patient and learn the math topics in short bursts.

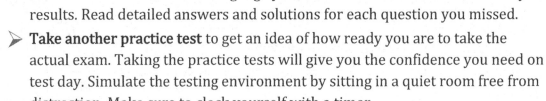

➢ Whenever you get a math problem wrong, **mark it off, and review it later** to make sure you understand the concept.

➢ Start each session by looking over the previous related material.

➢ Once you've reviewed the book's lessons, **take a practice test** at the back of the book to gauge your level of readiness. Then, review your results. Read detailed answers and solutions for each question you missed.

➢ **Take another practice test** to get an idea of how ready you are to take the actual exam. Taking the practice tests will give you the confidence you need on test day. Simulate the testing environment by sitting in a quiet room free from distraction. Make sure to clock yourself with a timer.

Looking for more?

Visit EffortlessMath.com/CollegeMathematics to find hundreds of College Math worksheets, video tutorials, practice tests, Math formulas, and much more.

No Registration Required.

Contents

CHAPTER

1 Fractions and Mixed Numbers

Math topics that you'll learn in this chapter:

- ☑ Simplifying Fractions
- ☑ Adding and Subtracting Fractions
- ☑ Multiplying and Dividing Fractions
- ☑ Adding Mixed Numbers
- ☑ Subtracting Mixed Numbers
- ☑ Multiplying Mixed Numbers
- ☑ Dividing Mixed Numbers

1

Simplifying Fractions

- A fraction contains two numbers separated by a bar between them. The bottom number, called the denominator, is the total number of equally divided portions in one whole. The top number, called the numerator, is how many portions you have. And the bar represents the operation of division.

- Simplifying a fraction means reducing it to the lowest terms. To simplify a fraction, evenly divide both the top and bottom of the fraction by $2, 3, 5, 7$, etc.

- Continue until you can't go any further.

Examples:

Example 1. Simplify $\frac{18}{30}$

Solution: To simplify $\frac{18}{30}$, find a number that both 18 and 30 are divisible by. Both are divisible by 6. Then: $\frac{18}{30} = \frac{18 \div 6}{30 \div 6} = \frac{3}{5}$

Example 2. Simplify $\frac{48}{80}$

Solution: To simplify $\frac{48}{80}$, find a number that both 48 and 80 are divisible by. Both are divisible by 8 and 16. Then: $\frac{48}{80} = \frac{48 \div 8}{80 \div 8} = \frac{6}{10}$, 6 and 10 are divisible by 2, then: $\frac{6}{10} = \frac{3}{5}$ or $\frac{48}{80} = \frac{48 \div 16}{80 \div 16} = \frac{3}{5}$

Example 3. Simplify $\frac{40}{120}$

Solution: To simplify $\frac{40}{120}$, find a number that both 40 and 120 are divisible by. Both are divisible by 40, then: $\frac{40}{120} = \frac{40 \div 40}{120 \div 40} = \frac{1}{3}$

Adding and Subtracting Fractions

- For "like" fractions (fractions with the same denominator), add or subtract the numerators (top numbers) and write the answer over the common denominator (bottom numbers).

- Adding and Subtracting fractions with the same denominator:

- $$\frac{a}{b} + \frac{c}{b} = \frac{a+c}{b} \qquad\qquad \frac{a}{b} - \frac{c}{b} = \frac{a-c}{b}$$

- Find equivalent fractions with the same denominator before you can add or subtract fractions with different denominators.

- Adding and Subtracting fractions with different denominators:

$$\frac{a}{b} + \frac{c}{d} = \frac{ad+bc}{bd} \qquad\qquad \frac{a}{b} - \frac{c}{d} = \frac{ad-bc}{bd}$$

Examples:

Example 1. Find the sum. $\frac{2}{3} + \frac{1}{2} =$

Solution: These two fractions are "unlike" fractions. (they have different denominators). Use this formula: $\frac{a}{b} + \frac{c}{d} = \frac{ad+cb}{bd}$

Then: $\frac{2}{3} + \frac{1}{2} = \frac{(2)(2)+(3)(1)}{3 \times 2} = \frac{4+3}{6} = \frac{7}{6}$

Example 2. Find the difference. $\frac{3}{5} - \frac{2}{7} =$

Solution: For "unlike" fractions, find equivalent fractions with the same denominator before you can add or subtract fractions with different denominators. Use this formula:

$\frac{a}{b} - \frac{c}{d} = \frac{ad-bc}{bd}$

$\frac{3}{5} - \frac{2}{7} = \frac{(3)(7)-(2)(5)}{5 \times 7} = \frac{21-10}{35} = \frac{11}{35}$

Multiplying and Dividing Fractions

- Multiplying fractions: multiply the top numbers and multiply the bottom numbers. Simplify if necessary. $\frac{a}{b} \times \frac{c}{d} = \frac{a \times c}{b \times d}$

- Dividing fractions: Keep, Change, Flip

- Keep the first fraction, change the division sign to multiplication, and flip the numerator and denominator of the second fraction. Then, solve!

$$\frac{a}{b} \div \frac{c}{d} = \frac{a}{b} \times \frac{d}{c} = \frac{a \times d}{b \times c}$$

Examples:

Example 1. Multiply. $\frac{2}{3} \times \frac{3}{5} =$

Solution: Multiply the top numbers and multiply the bottom numbers.
$\frac{2}{3} \times \frac{3}{5} = \frac{2 \times 3}{3 \times 5} = \frac{6}{15}$

Example 2. Solve. $\frac{3}{4} \div \frac{2}{5} =$

Solution: Keep the first fraction, change the division sign to multiplication, and flip the numerator and denominator of the second fraction.
Then: $\frac{3}{4} \div \frac{2}{5} = \frac{3}{4} \times \frac{5}{2} = \frac{3 \times 5}{4 \times 2} = \frac{15}{8}$

Example 3. Calculate. $\frac{4}{5} \times \frac{3}{4} =$

Solution: Multiply the top numbers and multiply the bottom numbers.
$\frac{4}{5} \times \frac{3}{4} = \frac{4 \times 3}{5 \times 4} = \frac{12}{20}$, simplify: $\frac{12}{20} = \frac{12 \div 4}{20 \div 4} = \frac{3}{5}$

Example 4. Solve. $\frac{5}{6} \div \frac{3}{7} =$

Solution: Keep the first fraction, change the division sign to multiplication, and flip the numerator and denominator of the second fraction.
Then: $\frac{5}{6} \div \frac{3}{7} = \frac{5}{6} \times \frac{7}{3} = \frac{5 \times 7}{6 \times 3} = \frac{35}{18}$

Adding Mixed Numbers

Use the following steps for adding mixed numbers:

- Add whole numbers of the mixed numbers.

- Add the fractions of the mixed numbers.

- Find the Least Common Denominator (LCD) if necessary.

- Add whole numbers and fractions.

- Write your answer in lowest terms.

Examples:

Example 1. Add mixed numbers. $2\frac{1}{2} + 1\frac{2}{3} =$

Solution: Let's rewriting our equation with parts separated, $2\frac{1}{2} + 1\frac{2}{3} = 2 + \frac{1}{2} + 1 + \frac{2}{3}$. Now, add whole number parts: $2 + 1 = 3$

Add the fraction parts $\frac{1}{2} + \frac{2}{3}$. Rewrite to solve with the equivalent fractions. $\frac{1}{2} + \frac{2}{3} = \frac{3}{6} + \frac{4}{6} = \frac{7}{6}$. The answer is an improper fraction (numerator is bigger than denominator). Convert the improper fraction into a mixed number: $\frac{7}{6} = 1\frac{1}{6}$. Now, combine the whole and fraction parts: $3 + 1\frac{1}{6} = 4\frac{1}{6}$

Example 2. Find the sum. $1\frac{3}{4} + 2\frac{1}{2} =$

Solution: Rewriting our equation with parts separated, $1 + \frac{3}{4} + 2 + \frac{1}{2}$. Add the whole number parts:

$1 + 2 = 3$. Add the fraction parts: $\frac{3}{4} + \frac{1}{2} = \frac{3}{4} + \frac{2}{4} = \frac{5}{4}$

Convert the improper fraction into a mixed number: $\frac{5}{4} = 1\frac{1}{4}$.

Now, combine the whole and fraction parts: $3 + 1\frac{1}{4} = 4\frac{1}{4}$

bit.ly/2M4oABB

Find more at

Subtracting Mixed Numbers

Use these steps for subtracting mixed numbers.

- Convert mixed numbers into improper fractions. $a\frac{c}{b} = \frac{ab+c}{b}$

- Find equivalent fractions with the same denominator for unlike fractions. (fractions with different denominators)

- Subtract the second fraction from the first one. $\frac{a}{b} - \frac{c}{d} = \frac{ad-bc}{bd}$

- Write your answer in lowest terms.

- If the answer is an improper fraction, convert it into a mixed number.

Examples:

Example 1. Subtract. $2\frac{1}{3} - 1\frac{1}{2} =$

Solution: Convert mixed numbers into fractions: $2\frac{1}{3} = \frac{2\times3+1}{3} = \frac{7}{3}$ and $1\frac{1}{2} = \frac{1\times2+1}{2} = \frac{3}{2}$

These two fractions are "unlike" fractions. (they have different denominators). Find equivalent fractions with the same denominator. Use this formula: $\frac{a}{b} - \frac{c}{d} = \frac{ad-bc}{bd}$

$$\frac{7}{3} - \frac{3}{2} = \frac{(7)(2)-(3)(3)}{3\times2} = \frac{14-9}{6} = \frac{5}{6}$$

Example 2. Subtract. $3\frac{4}{7} - 2\frac{3}{4} =$

Solution: Convert mixed numbers into fractions: $3\frac{4}{7} = \frac{3\times7+4}{7} = \frac{25}{7}$ and $2\frac{3}{4} = \frac{2\times4+3}{4} = \frac{11}{4}$

Then: $3\frac{4}{7} - 2\frac{3}{4} = \frac{25}{7} - \frac{11}{4} = \frac{(25)(4)-(11)(7)}{7\times4} = \frac{23}{28}$

Multiplying Mixed Numbers

Use the following steps for multiplying mixed numbers:

- Convert the mixed numbers into fractions. $a\frac{c}{b} = a + \frac{c}{b} = \frac{ab + c}{b}$

- Multiply fractions. $\frac{a}{b} \times \frac{c}{d} = \frac{a \times c}{b \times d}$

- Write your answer in lowest terms.

- If the answer is an improper fraction (numerator is bigger than denominator), convert it into a mixed number.

Examples:

Example 1. Multiply. $4\frac{1}{2} \times 2\frac{2}{5} =$

Solution: Convert mixed numbers into fractions, $4\frac{1}{2} = \frac{4 \times 2 + 1}{2} = \frac{9}{2}$ and

$$2\frac{2}{5} = \frac{2 \times 5 + 2}{5} = \frac{12}{5}$$

Apply the fractions rule for multiplication, $\frac{9}{2} \times \frac{12}{5} = \frac{9 \times 12}{2 \times 5} = \frac{108}{10}$

The answer is an improper fraction. Convert it into a mixed number. $\frac{108}{10} = 10\frac{4}{5}$

Example 2. Multiply. $3\frac{2}{3} \times 2\frac{5}{6} =$

Solution: Converting mixed numbers into fractions, $3\frac{2}{3} \times 2\frac{5}{6} = \frac{11}{3} \times \frac{17}{6}$

Apply the fractions rule for multiplication, $\frac{11}{3} \times \frac{17}{6} = \frac{11 \times 17}{3 \times 6} = \frac{187}{18} = 10\frac{7}{18}$

Example 3. Multiply mixed numbers. $5\frac{1}{4} \times 3\frac{3}{8} =$

Solution: Converting mixed numbers to fractions, $5\frac{1}{4} = \frac{21}{4}$ and $3\frac{3}{8} = \frac{27}{8}$. Multiply

two fractions:

$\frac{21}{4} \times \frac{27}{8} = \frac{21 \times 27}{4 \times 8} = \frac{567}{32} = 17\frac{23}{32}$

Find more at

bit.ly/3aPy7XJ

Dividing Mixed Numbers

Use the following steps for dividing mixed numbers:

- Convert the mixed numbers into fractions. $a\frac{c}{b} = a + \frac{c}{b} = \frac{ab+c}{b}$

- Divide fractions: Keep, Change, Flip: Keep the first fraction, change the division sign to multiplication, and flip the numerator and denominator of the second fraction. Then, solve! $\frac{a}{b} \div \frac{c}{d} = \frac{a}{b} \times \frac{d}{c} = \frac{a \times d}{b \times c}$

- Write your answer in lowest terms.

- If the answer is an improper fraction (numerator is bigger than denominator), convert it into a mixed number.

Examples:

Example 1. Solve. $2\frac{1}{3} \div 1\frac{1}{2}$

Solution: Convert mixed numbers into fractions: $2\frac{1}{3} = \frac{2 \times 3 + 1}{3} = \frac{7}{3}$ and $1\frac{1}{2} = \frac{1 \times 2 + 1}{2} = \frac{3}{2}$
Keep, Change, Flip: $\frac{7}{3} \div \frac{3}{2} = \frac{7}{3} \times \frac{2}{3} = \frac{7 \times 2}{3 \times 3} = \frac{14}{9}$. The answer is an improper fraction. Convert it into a mixed number: $\frac{14}{9} = 1\frac{5}{9}$

Example 2. Solve. $3\frac{3}{4} \div 2\frac{2}{5}$

Solution: Convert mixed numbers to fractions, then solve:
$3\frac{3}{4} \div 2\frac{2}{5} = \frac{15}{4} \div \frac{12}{5} = \frac{15}{4} \times \frac{5}{12} = \frac{75}{48} = 1\frac{9}{16}$

Example 3. Solve. $2\frac{4}{5} \div 1\frac{2}{3}$

Solution: Converting mixed numbers to fractions: $2\frac{4}{5} \div 1\frac{2}{3} = \frac{14}{5} \div \frac{5}{3}$
Keep, Change, Flip: $\frac{14}{5} \div \frac{5}{3} = \frac{14}{5} \times \frac{3}{5} = \frac{14 \times 3}{5 \times 5} = \frac{42}{25} = 1\frac{17}{25}$

Chapter 1: Practices

✍ Simplify each fraction.

1) $\frac{2}{8} = \frac{1}{4}$

2) $\frac{5}{15} = \frac{1}{3}$

3) $\frac{10}{90} = \frac{1}{9}$

4) $\frac{12}{16} = \frac{3}{4}$

5) $\frac{25}{45} = \frac{5}{9}$

6) $\frac{42}{54} = \frac{7}{9}$

7) $\frac{48}{60} = \frac{4}{5}$

8) $\frac{52}{169} = \frac{4}{13}$

✍ Find the sum or difference.

9) $\frac{3}{10} + \frac{2}{10} = \frac{5}{10} = \frac{1}{2}$

10) $\frac{4}{9} - \frac{1}{9} = \frac{3}{9} = \frac{1}{3}$

11) $\frac{2}{3} + \frac{6}{15} = \frac{16}{15} = 1\frac{1}{15}$

12) $\frac{17}{24} - \frac{5}{8} = \frac{2}{24} = \frac{1}{12}$

13) $\frac{7}{54} - \frac{1}{9} = \frac{1}{54}$

14) $\frac{4}{5} - \frac{1}{6} = \frac{19}{30}$

15) $\frac{6}{7} - \frac{3}{8} = \frac{27}{56}$

16) $\frac{2}{13} + \frac{1}{4} = \frac{21}{52}$

✍ Find the products or quotients.

17) $\frac{2}{9} \div \frac{4}{3} = \frac{6}{36} = \frac{1}{6}$

18) $\frac{14}{5} \div \frac{28}{35} = \frac{490}{140} = \frac{7}{2} = 3\frac{1}{2}$

19) $\frac{9}{25} \times \frac{5}{27} = \frac{45}{675} = \frac{1}{135}$

20) $\frac{65}{72} \times \frac{12}{153} = \frac{13}{18}$

✍ Find the sum.

21) $2\frac{1}{5} + 1\frac{2}{5} = 3\frac{3}{5}$

22) $5\frac{1}{9} + 2\frac{7}{9} = 7\frac{8}{9}$

23) $2\frac{3}{4} + 1\frac{1}{8} = \frac{31}{8} = 3\frac{7}{8}$

24) $2\frac{2}{7} + 4\frac{1}{21} = \frac{133}{21} = 6\frac{7}{21} = 6\frac{1}{3}$

25) $5\frac{3}{5} + 1\frac{4}{9} = 6\frac{47}{45} = 7\frac{2}{45}$

26) $3\frac{3}{11} + 4\frac{6}{7} = 7\frac{87}{77} = 8\frac{10}{77}$

Effortless
Math
Education

✎ **Find the difference**.

27) $5\frac{1}{3} - 4\frac{2}{3} = \frac{2}{3}$

28) $4\frac{7}{10} - 1\frac{3}{10} = 3\frac{4}{10} = 3\frac{2}{5}$

29) $3\frac{1}{3} - 2\frac{2}{9} = \frac{10}{9} = 1\frac{1}{9}$

30) $6\frac{1}{2} - 3\frac{1}{3} = \frac{19}{6} = 3\frac{1}{6}$

31) $4\frac{3}{4} - 2\frac{1}{28} = 2\frac{20}{28} = 2\frac{5}{7}$

32) $4\frac{2}{7} - 3\frac{1}{6} = 1\frac{5}{42}$

33) $5\frac{3}{10} - 3\frac{3}{4} = 1\frac{11}{20}$

34) $6\frac{9}{20} - 2\frac{1}{3} = 4\frac{7}{60}$

✎ **Find the products.**

35) $1\frac{1}{2} \times 2\frac{3}{7} = \frac{51}{14} = 3\frac{9}{14}$

36) $1\frac{3}{4} \times 1\frac{3}{5} = \frac{56}{20} = 2\frac{16}{20} = 2\frac{4}{5}$

37) $4\frac{1}{2} \times 1\frac{5}{6} = \frac{99}{12} = 8\frac{3}{12} = 8\frac{1}{4}$

38) $1\frac{2}{7} \times 3\frac{1}{5} = \frac{144}{35} = 4\frac{4}{35}$

39) $2\frac{1}{5} \times 5\frac{1}{2} = \frac{121}{10} = 12\frac{1}{10}$

40) $2\frac{1}{2} \times 4\frac{4}{5} = \frac{120}{10} = 12$

41) $3\frac{1}{5} \times 4\frac{1}{2} = \frac{144}{10} = 14\frac{4}{10} = 14\frac{2}{5}$

42) $4\frac{9}{10} \times 4\frac{1}{2} = \frac{441}{20} = 22\frac{1}{20}$

✎ **Solve.**

43) $1\frac{1}{3} \div 1\frac{2}{3} = \frac{12}{15} = \frac{4}{5}$

44) $2\frac{1}{4} \div 1\frac{1}{2} = \frac{18}{12} = 1\frac{1}{2}$

45) $5\frac{1}{3} \div 3\frac{1}{2} = \frac{32}{21} = 1\frac{11}{21}$

46) $3\frac{2}{7} \div 1\frac{1}{8} = \frac{184}{63} = 2\frac{58}{63}$

47) $4\frac{1}{5} \div 2\frac{2}{3} = \frac{63}{40} = 1\frac{23}{40}$

48) $1\frac{2}{3} \div 1\frac{3}{8} = \frac{40}{33} = 1\frac{7}{33}$

49) $4\frac{1}{2} \div 2\frac{2}{3} = \frac{27}{16} = 1\frac{11}{16}$

50) $1\frac{2}{11} \div 1\frac{1}{8} = \frac{104}{99} = 1\frac{5}{99}$

$$\frac{19}{4} - \frac{57}{28}$$

$$\frac{133}{28} - \frac{57}{28} = \frac{76}{28} = 2\frac{20}{28} = 2\frac{5}{7}$$

$$\frac{2128}{784}$$

$$\frac{53}{10} - \frac{15}{4}$$

$$\frac{106}{20} - \frac{75}{20} = \frac{31}{20} = 1\frac{11}{20}$$

$$1.91$$
$$5.20$$
$$3820$$
$$95500$$
$$99320$$

④

$$12.40$$
$$4.20$$
$$24800$$
$$496000$$
$$520800$$

$$\frac{3}{2} \qquad \frac{17}{7}$$

$$\begin{array}{r} 9.2 \\ 2\overline{)18.4} \\ 18 \\ 4 \end{array}$$

$$\frac{9}{7} \times \frac{16}{5} \qquad \frac{144}{35}$$

$$\frac{16}{5} \times \frac{9}{2} \qquad \frac{144}{10}$$

$$\begin{array}{r} 22.875 \\ 16\overline{)366} \\ 32 \\ 46 \\ 32 \\ 140 \\ 128 \\ 120 \\ 112 \\ 80 \\ 80 \end{array}$$

$$\frac{49}{10} \times \frac{9}{2} \qquad \frac{441}{20} \qquad 22\frac{1}{20}$$

$$\begin{array}{r} 62.05 \\ 14\overline{)24.32} \end{array}$$

$$\begin{array}{r} 8.0 \\ 3\overline{)24} \end{array}$$

$$\begin{array}{r} 2.4 \\ 2\overline{)4.8} \end{array}$$

$$4$$

$$3.65$$
$$140$$
$$14600$$
$$36500$$
$$51100$$

Chapter 1: Answers

1) $\frac{1}{4}$

2) $\frac{1}{3}$

3) $\frac{1}{9}$

4) $\frac{3}{4}$

5) $\frac{5}{9}$

6) $\frac{7}{9}$

7) $\frac{4}{5}$

8) $\frac{4}{13}$

9) $\frac{1}{2}$

10) $\frac{1}{3}$

11) $\frac{16}{15} = 1\frac{1}{15}$

12) $\frac{1}{12}$

13) $\frac{1}{54}$

14) $\frac{19}{30}$

15) $\frac{27}{56}$

16) $\frac{21}{52}$

17) $\frac{1}{6}$

18) $\frac{7}{2} = 3\frac{1}{2}$

19) $\frac{1}{15}$

20) $\frac{13}{18}$

21) $3\frac{3}{5}$

22) $7\frac{8}{9}$

23) $3\frac{7}{8}$

24) $6\frac{1}{3}$

25) $7\frac{2}{45}$

26) $8\frac{10}{77}$

27) $\frac{2}{3}$

28) $3\frac{2}{5}$

29) $1\frac{1}{9}$

30) $3\frac{1}{6}$

31) $2\frac{5}{7}$

32) $1\frac{5}{42}$

33) $1\frac{11}{20}$

34) $4\frac{7}{60}$

35) $3\frac{9}{14}$

36) $2\frac{4}{5}$

37) $8\frac{1}{4}$

38) $4\frac{4}{35}$

39) $12\frac{1}{10}$

40) 12

41) $14\frac{2}{5}$

42) $22\frac{1}{20}$

43) $\frac{4}{5}$

44) $1\frac{1}{2}$

45) $1\frac{11}{21}$

46) $2\frac{58}{63}$

47) $1\frac{23}{40}$

48) $1\frac{7}{33}$

49) $1\frac{11}{16}$

50) $1\frac{5}{99}$

Effortless
Math
Education

EffortlessMath.com

CHAPTER

2 Decimals

Math topics that you'll learn in this chapter:

- ☑ Comparing Decimals
- ☑ Rounding Decimals
- ☑ Adding and Subtracting Decimals
- ☑ Multiplying and Dividing Decimals

13

Comparing Decimals

- A decimal is a fraction written in a special form. For example, instead of writing $\frac{1}{2}$ you can write 0.5

- A Decimal Number contains a Decimal Point. It separates the whole number part from the fractional part of a decimal number.

- Let's review decimal place values: Example: 53.9861

5: tens   3: ones   9: tenths

8: hundredths   6: thousandths   1: tens thousandths

- To compare decimals, compare each digit of two decimals in the same place value. Start from left. Compare hundreds, tens, ones, tenth, hundredth, etc.

- To compare numbers, use these symbols:

Equal to =,   Less than <,   Greater than >

Greater than or equal ≥,   Less than or equal ≤

Examples:

Example 1. Compare 0.03 and 0.30.

Solution: 0.30 is greater than 0.03, because the tenth place of 0.30 is 3, but the tenth place of 0.03 is zero. Then: $0.03 < 0.30$

Example 2. Compare 0.0217 and 0.217.

Solution: 0.217 is greater than 0.0217, because the tenth place of 0.217 is 2, but the tenth place of 0.0217 is zero. Then: $0.0217 < 0.217$

Rounding Decimals

- We can round decimals to a certain accuracy or number of decimal places. This is used to make calculations easier to do and results easier to understand when exact values are not too important.

- First, you'll need to remember your place values: For example: 12.4869

  1: tens   2: ones   4: tenths

  8: hundredths   6: thousandths   9: tens thousandths

- To round a decimal, first find the place value you'll round to.

- Find the digit to the right of the place value you're rounding to. If it is 5 or bigger, add 1 to the place value you're rounding to and remove all digits on its right side. If the digit to the right of the place value is less than 5, keep the place value and remove all digits on the right.

Examples:

Example 1. Round 4.3679 to the thousandth place value.

Solution: First, look at the next place value to the right, (tens thousandths). It's 9 and it is greater than 5. Thus add 1 to the digit in the thousandth place. The thousandth place is 7. $\rightarrow 7 + 1 = 8$, then,
The answer is 4.368

Example 2. Round 1.5237 to the nearest hundredth.

Solution: First, look at the digit to the right of hundredth (thousandths place value). It's 3 and it is less than 5, thus remove all the digits to the right of hundredth place. Then, the answer is 1.52.

Adding and Subtracting Decimals

- Line up the decimal numbers.

- Add zeros to have the same number of digits for both numbers if necessary.

- Remember your place values: For example: 73.5196

    7: tens   3: ones   5: tenths

    1: hundredths   9: thousandths   6: tens thousandths

- Add or subtract using column addition or subtraction.

Examples:

Example 1. Add. $1.7 + 4.12$

Solution: First, line up the numbers: $\begin{array}{r} 1.7 \\ +\,4.12 \\ \hline \end{array} \to$ Add a zero to have the same number of digits for both numbers. $\begin{array}{r} 1.70 \\ +\,4.12 \\ \hline \end{array} \to$ Start with the hundredths place: $0 + 2 = 2$, $\begin{array}{r} 1.70 \\ +\,4.12 \\ \hline 2 \end{array} \to$ Continue with tenths place: $7 + 1 = 8$, $\begin{array}{r} 1.70 \\ +\,4.12 \\ \hline .82 \end{array} \to$ Add the ones place: $4 + 1 = 5$, $\begin{array}{r} 1.70 \\ +\,4.12 \\ \hline 5.82 \end{array}$

Example 2. Find the difference. $5.58 - 4.23$

Solution: First, line up the numbers: $\begin{array}{r} 5.58 \\ -\,4.23 \\ \hline \end{array} \to$ Start with the hundredths place: $8 - 3 = 5$, $\begin{array}{r} 5.58 \\ -\,4.23 \\ \hline 5 \end{array} \to$ Continue with tenths place. $5 - 2 = 3$, $\begin{array}{r} 5.58 \\ -\,4.23 \\ \hline .35 \end{array} \to$ Subtract the ones place. $5 - 4 = 1$, $\begin{array}{r} 5.58 \\ -\,4.23 \\ \hline 1.35 \end{array}$

Multiplying and Dividing Decimals

For multiplying decimals:

- Ignore the decimal point and set up and multiply the numbers as you do with whole numbers.

- Count the total number of decimal places in both of the factors.

- Place the decimal point in the product.

For dividing decimals:

- If the divisor is not a whole number, move the decimal point to the right to make it a whole number. Do the same for the dividend.

- Divide similar to whole numbers.

Examples:

Example 1. Find the product. $0.65 \times 0.24 =$

Solution: Set up and multiply the numbers as you do with whole numbers. Line up the numbers: $\frac{65}{\times 24}$ → Start with the ones place then continue with other digits $\rightarrow \frac{\begin{array}{r} 65 \\ \times 24 \end{array}}{1,560}$. Count the total number of decimal places in both of the factors. There are four decimals digits. (two for each factor 0.65 and 0.24) Then: $0.65 \times 0.24 = 0.1560$

Example 2. Find the quotient. $1.20 \div 0.4 =$

Solution: The divisor is not a whole number. Multiply it by 10 to get 4: → $0.4 \times 10 = 4$
Do the same for the dividend to get 12. → $1.20 \times 10 = 12$
Now, divide $12 \div 4 = 3$. The answer is 3.

bit.ly/34DZ0cS

Find more at

Chapter 2: Practices

✍ Compare. Use >, =, and <

1) 0.5 < 0.6

2) 0.9 > 0.8

3) 0.1 < 0.2

4) 0.02 < 0.06

5) 0.05 < 0.08

6) 0.12 > 0.09

7) 3.2 > 2.5

8) 4.8 < 8.4

9) 0.005 < 0.05

10) 2.02 < 20.020

11) 55.100 = 55.10

12) 0.44 = 0.440

13) 6.01 = 6.0100

14) 0.77 < 77.0

✍ Round each decimal to the nearest whole number.

15) 5.8   6

16) 6.4   6

17) 12.3   12

18) 9.2   9

19) 7.6   8

20) 22.4   22

21) 6.8   7

22) 15.9   16

23) 13.41   13

24) 16.78   17

25) 67.58   68

26) 42.67   43

27) 55.89   56

28) 14.32   14

29) 78.88   79

30) 98.29   98

Effortless Math Education

✎ Find the sum or difference.

31) $12.1 + 36.2 =$ 48.3

32) $56.3 - 22.2 =$ 34.1

33) $45.1 + 12.8 =$ 57.9

34) $27.9 - 16.4 =$ 11.5

35) $98.8 - 56.6 =$ 42.2

36) $28.45 + 13.22 =$ 41.67

37) $16.78 + 45.11 =$ 61.89

38) $86.16 - 72.12 =$ 14.04

39) $96.23 - 28.32 =$ 67.91

40) $57.33 + 67.46 =$ 124.79

41) $46.26 - 39.49 =$ 6.87

42) $44.95 + 76.53 =$ 121.48

43) $79.37 - 52.89 =$ 26.48

44) $19.99 + 28.7 =$ 48.69

45) $83.48 - 49.3 =$ 34.18

46) $19.6 + 42.98 =$ 62.58

✎ Find the product or quotient.

47) $3.3 \times 0.2 =$ .66

48) $2.4 \div 0.3 =$ 8

49) $8.1 \times 1.4 =$ 11.34

50) $4.8 \div 0.2 =$ 24

51) $4.1 \times 0.3 =$ 1.23

52) $8.6 \div 0.2 =$ 43

53) $9.9 \times 0.8 =$ 7.92

54) $1.84 \div 0.2 =$ 9.2

55) $2.1 \times 8.4 =$ 17.64

56) $1.6 \times 4.5 =$ 7.2

57) $9.2 \times 3.1 =$ 28.52

58) $36.6 \div 1.6 =$ 22.875

59) $1.91 \times 5.2 =$ 9.932

60) $3.65 \times 1.4 =$ 5.11

61) $24.82 \div 0.4 =$ 62.05

62) $12.4 \times 4.20 =$ 52.08

Effortless
Math
Education

Chapter 2: Answers

1)	<	22)	16	43)	26.48
2)	>	23)	13	44)	48.69
3)	<	24)	17	45)	34.18
4)	<	25)	68	46)	62.58
5)	<	26)	43	47)	0.66
6)	>	27)	56	48)	8
7)	>	28)	14	49)	11.34
8)	<	29)	79	50)	24
9)	<	30)	98	51)	1.23
10)	<	31)	48.3	52)	43
11)	=	32)	34.1	53)	7.92
12)	=	33)	57.9	54)	9.2
13)	=	34)	11.5	55)	17.64
14)	<	35)	42.2	56)	7.2
15)	6	36)	41.67	57)	28.52
16)	6	37)	61.89	58)	22.875
17)	12	38)	14.04	59)	9.932
18)	9	39)	67.91	60)	5.11
19)	8	40)	124.79	61)	62.05
20)	22	41)	6.77	62)	52.08
21)	7	42)	121.48		

3 Integers and Order of Operations

Math topics that you'll learn in this chapter:

- ☑ Adding and Subtracting Integers
- ☑ Multiplying and Dividing Integers
- ☑ Order of Operations
- ☑ Integers and Absolute Value

21

Adding and Subtracting Integers

- Integers include zero, counting numbers, and the negative of the counting numbers. $\{\dots, -3, -2, -1, 0, 1, 2, 3, \dots\}$

- Add a positive integer by moving to the right on the number line. (you will get a bigger number)

- Add a negative integer by moving to the left on the number line. (you will get a smaller number)

- Subtract an integer by adding its opposite.

Examples:

Example 1. Solve. $(-2) - (-8) =$

Solution: Keep the first number and convert the sign of the second number to its opposite. (change subtraction into addition. Then: $(-2) + 8 = 6$

Example 2. Solve. $4 + (5 - 10) =$

Solution: First, subtract the numbers in brackets, $5 - 10 = -5$.
Then: $4 + (-5) = \rightarrow$ change addition into subtraction: $4 - 5 = -1$

Example 3. Solve. $(9 - 14) + 15 =$

Solution: First, subtract the numbers in brackets, $9 - 14 = -5$
Then: $-5 + 15 = \rightarrow -5 + 15 = 10$

Example 4. Solve. $12 + (-3 - 10) =$

Solution: First, subtract the numbers in brackets, $-3 - 10 = -13$
Then: $12 + (-13) = \rightarrow$ change addition into subtraction: $12 - 13 = -1$

Multiplying and Dividing Integers

Use the following rules for multiplying and dividing integers:

- (negative) × (negative) = positive

- (negative) ÷ (negative) = positive

- (negative) × (positive) = negative

- (negative) ÷ (positive) = negative

- (positive) × (positive) = positive

- (positive) ÷ (negative) = negative

Examples:

Example 1. Solve. $3 \times (-4) =$

Solution: Use this rule: (positive) × (negative) = negative.
Then: $(3) \times (-4) = -12$

Example 2. Solve. $(-3) + (-24 \div 3) =$

Solution: First, divide -24 by 3, the numbers in brackets, use this rule:
(negative) ÷ (positive) = negative. Then: $-24 \div 3 = -8$
$(-3) + (-24 \div 3) = (-3) + (-8) = -3 - 8 = -11$

Example 3. Solve. $(12 - 15) \times (-2) =$

Solution: First, subtract the numbers in brackets,
$12 - 15 = -3 \rightarrow (-3) \times (-2) =$
Now use this rule: (negative) × (negative) = positive $\rightarrow (-3) \times (-2) = 6$

Example 4. Solve. $(12 - 8) \div (-4) =$

Solution: First, subtract the numbers in brackets,
$12 - 8 = 4 \rightarrow (4) \div (-4) =$
Now use this rule: (positive) ÷ (negative) = negative $\rightarrow (4) \div (-4) = -1$

Find more at bit.ly/3pjQW98

Order of Operations

- In Mathematics, "operations" are addition, subtraction, multiplication, division, exponentiation (written as b^n), and grouping.

- When there is more than one math operation in an expression, use PEMDAS: (to memorize this rule, remember the phrase "Please Excuse My Dear Aunt Sally".)

❖ Parentheses

❖ Exponents

❖ Multiplication and Division (from left to right)

❖ Addition and Subtraction (from left to right)

Examples:

Example 1. Calculate. $(2 + 6) \div (2^2 \div 4) =$

Solution: First, simplify inside parentheses:
$(8) \div (4 \div 4) = (8) \div (1)$, Then: $(8) \div (1) = 8$

Example 2. Solve. $(6 \times 5) - (14 - 5) =$

Solution: First, calculate within parentheses: $(6 \times 5) - (14 - 5) = (30) - (9)$, Then: $(30) - (9) = 21$

Example 3. Calculate. $-4[(3 \times 6) \div (3^2 \times 2)] =$

Solution: First, calculate within parentheses:
$-4[(18) \div (9 \times 2)] = -4[(18) \div (18)] = -4[1]$
multiply -4 and 1. Then: $-4[1] = -4$

Example 4. Solve. $(28 \div 7) + (-19 + 3) =$

Solution: First, calculate within parentheses:
$(28 \div 7) + (-19 + 3) = (4) + (-16)$ Then: $(4) - (16) = -12$

Integers and Absolute Value

- The absolute value of a number is its distance from zero, in either direction, on the number line. For example, the distance of 9 and −9 from zero on number line is 9.

- The absolute value of an integer is the numerical value without its sign. (negative or positive)

- The vertical bar is used for absolute value as in $|x|$.

- The absolute value of a number is never negative; because it only shows, "how far the number is from zero".

Examples:

Example 1. Calculate. $|14 − 2| \times 5 =$

Solution: First, solve $|14 − 2|$, $\rightarrow |14 − 2| = |12|$, the absolute value of 12 is 12, $|12| = 12$ Then: $12 \times 5 = 60$

Example 2. Solve. $\frac{|-24|}{4} \times |5 − 7| =$

Solution: First, find $|-24|$, $\rightarrow$ the absolute value of −24 is 24,
Then: $|-24| = 24$, $\frac{24}{4} \times |5 − 7| =$
Now, calculate $|5 − 7|$, $\rightarrow |5 − 7| = |-2|$, the absolute value of −2 is 2. $|-2| = 2$
then: $\frac{24}{4} \times 2 = 6 \times 2 = 12$

Example 3. Solve. $|8 − 2| \times \frac{|-4 \times 7|}{2} =$

Solution: First, calculate $|8 − 2|$, $\rightarrow |8 − 2| = |6|$, the absolute value of 6 is 6, $|6| = 6$. Then: $6 \times \frac{|-4 \times 7|}{2}$
Now calculate $|-4 \times 7|$, $\rightarrow |-4 \times 7| = |-28|$, the absolute value of −28 is 28, $|-28| = 28$ Then: $6 \times \frac{28}{2} = 6 \times 14 = 84$

Chapter 3: Practices

✍ Find each sum or difference.

1) $-9 + 16 = 7$

2) $-18 - 6 = -24$

3) $-24 + 10 = -14$

4) $30 + (-5) = 25$

5) $15 + (-3) = 12$

6) $(-13) + (-4) = -17$

7) $25 + (3 - 10) = 18$

8) $12 - (-6 + 9) = 9$

9) $5 - (-2 + 7) = 0$

10) $(-11) + (-5 + 6) = -10$

11) $(-3) + (9 - 16) = -10$

12) $(-8) - (13 + 4) = -25$

13) $(-7 + 9) - 39 = -37$

14) $(-30 + 6) - 14 = -38$

15) $(-5 + 9) + (-3 + 7) = 8$

16) $(8 - 19) - (-4 + 12) = -19$

17) $(-9 + 2) - (6 - 7) = -6$

18) $(-12 - 5) - (-4 - 14) = 1$

✍ Solve.

19) $3 \times (-6) = -18$

20) $(-32) \div 4 = -8$

21) $(-5) \times 4 = -20$

22) $(25) \div (-5) = -5$

23) $(-72) \div 8 = -9$

24) $(-2) \times (-6) \times 5 = 60$

25) $(-2) \times 3 \times (-7) = 42$

26) $(-1) \times (-3) \times (-5) = -15$

27) $(-2) \times (-3) \times (-6) = -36$

28) $(-12 + 3) \times (-5) = 45$

29) $(-3 + 4) \times (-11) = -11$

30) $(-9) \times (6 - 5) = -9$

31) $(-3 - 7) \times (-6) = 60$

32) $(-7 + 3) \times (-9 + 6) = 12$

33) $(-15) \div (-17 + 12) = 3$

34) $(-3 - 2) \times (-9 + 7) = 10$

35) $(-15 + 31) \div (-2) = -8$

36) $(-64) \div (-16 + 8) = 8$

✐ Evaluate each expression.

37) $3 + (2 \times 5) = 13$

38) $(5 \times 4) - 7 = 13$

39) $(-9 \times 2) + 6 = -12$

40) $(7 \times 3) - (-5) = 26$

41) $(-8) + (2 \times 7) = 6$

42) $(9 - 6) + (3 \times 4) = 15$

43) $(-19 + 5) + (6 \times 2) = -2$

44) $(32 \div 4) + (1 - 13) = -4$

45) $(-36 \div 6) - (12 + 3) = -21$

46) $(-16 + 5) - (54 \div 9) = -17$

47) $(-20 + 4) - (35 \div 5) = -23$

48) $(42 \div 7) + (2 \times 3) = 12$

49) $(28 \div 4) + (2 \times 6) = 19$

50) $2[(3 \times 3) - (4 \times 5)] = -22$

51) $3[(2 \times 8) + (4 \times 3)] = 84$

52) $2[(9 \times 3) - (6 \times 4)] = 6$

53) $4[(4 \times 8) \div (4 \times 4)] = 8$

54) $-5[(10 \times 8) \div (5 \times 8)] = -10$

✐ Find the answers.

55) $|-5| + |7 - 10| = 8$

56) $|-4 + 6| + |-2| = 4$

57) $|-9| + |1 - 9| = 17$

58) $|-7| - |8 - 12| = 3$

59) $|9 - 11| + |8 - 15| = 9$

60) $|-7 + 10| - |-8 + 3| = -2$

61) $|-12 + 6| - |3 - 9| = 0$

62) $5 + |2 - 6| + |3 - 4| = 10$

63) $-4 + |2 - 6| + |1 - 9| = 8$

64) $|-6| \times |-7| + |2 - 8| = 48$

65) $|-12| \times |-3| + |4 - 28| = 60$

66) $|4 \times (-2)| \times |-9| = 72$

67) $|-3 \times 2| \times |-5| = 30$

68) $|3 - 12| - |-3 \times 7| = -12$

69) $|-9| + |-7 \times 5| = 44$

70) $|-11| + |-6 \times 4| = 35$

71) $|-4 \times 2 + 6| \times |-2 \times 8| = 32$

72) $|-1 \times 5 + 2| \times |-4| = 12$

| Effortless |
| Math |
| Education |

Chapter 3: Answers

1) 7	25) 42	49) 19
2) −24	26) −15	50) −22
3) −14	27) −36	51) 84
4) 25	28) 45	52) 6
5) 12	29) −11	53) 8
6) −17	30) −9	54) −10
7) 18	31) 60	55) 8
8) 9	32) 12	56) 4
9) 0	33) 3	57) 17
10) −10	34) 10	58) 3
11) −10	35) −8	59) 9
12) −25	36) 8	60) −2
13) −37	37) 13	61) 0
14) −38	38) 13	62) 10
15) 8	39) −12	63) 8
16) −19	40) 26	64) 48
17) −6	41) 6	65) 60
18) 1	42) 15	66) 72
19) −18	43) −2	67) 30
20) −8	44) −4	68) −12
21) −20	45) −21	69) 44
22) −5	46) −17	70) 35
23) −9	47) −23	71) 32
24) 60	48) 12	72) 12

CHAPTER

4 Ratios and Proportions

Math topics that you'll learn in this chapter:

- ☑ Simplifying Ratios
- ☑ Proportional Ratios
- ☑ Similarity and Ratios

29

Simplifying Ratios

- Ratios are used to make comparisons between two numbers.

- Ratios can be written as a fraction, using the word "to", or with a colon. Example: $\frac{3}{4}$ or "3 to 4" or 3:4

- You can calculate equivalent ratios by multiplying or dividing both sides of the ratio by the same number.

Examples:

Example 1. Simplify. $8:2 =$

Solution: Both numbers 8 and 2 are divisible by 2 $\Rightarrow 8 \div 2 = 4$, $4 \div 2 = 2$, Then: $8:2 = 4:1$

Example 2. Simplify. $\frac{9}{33} =$

Solution: Both numbers 9 and 33 are divisible by 3, $\Rightarrow 33 \div 3 = 11$, $9 \div 3 = 3$, Then: $\frac{9}{33} = \frac{3}{11}$

Example 3. There are 24 students in a class and 10 are girls. Write the ratio of girls to boys.

Solution: Subtract 10 from 24 to find the number of boys in the class.
$24 - 10 = 14$. There are 14 boys in the class. So, the ratio of girls to boys is $10:14$.
Now, simplify this ratio. Both 14 and 10 are divisible by 2.
Then: $14 \div 2 = 7$, and $10 \div 2 = 5$. In the simplest form, this ratio is $5:7$

Example 4. A recipe calls for butter and sugar in the ratio $3:4$. If you're using 9 cups of butter, how many cups of sugar should you use?

Solution: Since you use 9 cups of butter, or 3 times as much, you need to multiply the amount of sugar by 3. Then: $4 \times 3 = 12$. So, you need to use 12 cups of sugar. You can solve this using equivalent fractions: $\frac{3}{4} = \frac{9}{12}$

Proportional Ratios

- Two ratios are proportional if they represent the same relationship.

- A proportion means that two ratios are equal. It can be written in two ways: $\dfrac{a}{b} = \dfrac{c}{d}$ $a : b = c : d$

- The proportion $\dfrac{a}{b} = \dfrac{c}{d}$ can be written as: $a \times d = c \times b$

Examples:

Example 1. Solve this proportion for x. $\dfrac{2}{5} = \dfrac{6}{x}$

Solution: Use cross multiplication: $\dfrac{2}{5} = \dfrac{6}{x} \Rightarrow 2 \times x = 6 \times 5 \Rightarrow 2x = 30$

Divide both sides by 2 to find x: $x = \dfrac{30}{2} \Rightarrow x = 15$

Example 2. If a box contains red and blue balls in ratio of $3 : 5$ red to blue, how many red balls are there if 45 blue balls are in the box?

Solution: Write a proportion and solve. $\dfrac{3}{5} = \dfrac{x}{45}$

Use cross multiplication: $3 \times 45 = 5 \times x \Rightarrow 135 = 5x$

Divide to find x: $x = \dfrac{135}{5} \Rightarrow x = 27$. There are 27 red balls in the box.

Example 3. Solve this proportion for x. $\dfrac{4}{9} = \dfrac{16}{x}$

Solution: Use cross multiplication: $\dfrac{4}{9} = \dfrac{16}{x} \Rightarrow 4 \times x = 9 \times 16 \Rightarrow 4x = 144$

Divide to find x: $x = \dfrac{144}{4} \Rightarrow x = 36$

Example 4. Solve this proportion for x. $\dfrac{5}{7} = \dfrac{20}{x}$

Solution: Use cross multiplication: $\dfrac{5}{7} = \dfrac{20}{x} \Rightarrow 5 \times x = 7 \times 20 \Rightarrow 5x = 140$

Divide to find x: $x = \dfrac{140}{5} \Rightarrow x = 28$

Similarity and Ratios

- Two figures are similar if they have the same shape.

- Two or more figures are similar if the corresponding angles are equal, and the corresponding sides are in proportion.

Examples:

Example 1. The following triangles are similar. What is the value of the unknown side?

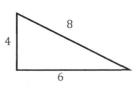

Solution: Find the corresponding sides and write a proportion.

$\frac{8}{20} = \frac{6}{x}$. Now, use the cross-product to solve for x:

$\frac{8}{20} = \frac{6}{x} \Rightarrow 8 \times x = 20 \times 6 \Rightarrow 8x = 120$.

Divide both sides by 8. Then: $8x = 120 \Rightarrow x = \frac{120}{8} \Rightarrow x = 15$.

The missing side is 15.

Example 2. Two rectangles are similar. The first is 5 feet wide and 15 feet long. The second is 10 feet wide. What is the length of the second rectangle?

Solution: Let's put x for the length of the second rectangle. Since two rectangles are similar, their corresponding sides are in proportion. Write a proportion and solve for the missing number.

$\frac{5}{10} = \frac{15}{x} \rightarrow 5x = 10 \times 15 \rightarrow 5x = 150 \rightarrow x = \frac{150}{5} = 30$

The length of the second rectangle is 30 feet.

Chapter 4: Practices

✎ Reduce each ratio.

1) $2:18 = \underline{1}:\underline{9}$

2) $5:35 = \underline{1}:\underline{7}$

3) $8:72 = \underline{1}:\underline{9}$

4) $24:36 = \underline{2}:\underline{3}$

5) $25:40 = \underline{5}:\underline{8}$

6) $40:72 = \underline{5}:\underline{9}$

7) $28:63 = \underline{4}:\underline{9}$

8) $18:81 = \underline{2}:\underline{9}$

9) $13:52 = \underline{1}:\underline{4}$

10) $56:72 = \underline{7}:\underline{9}$

11) $42:63 = \underline{2}:\underline{3}$

12) $32:96 = \underline{1}:\underline{3}$

✎ Solve.

13) Bob has 16 red cards and 20 green cards. What is the ratio of Bob's red cards to his green cards? $\underline{4:5}$

14) In a party, 34 soft drinks are required for every 20 guests. If there are 260 guests, how many soft drinks are required? $\underline{442}$ $\frac{20}{34} = \frac{260}{x}$

15) Sara has 56 blue pens and 28 black pens. What is the ratio of Sara's black pens to her blue pens? $\underline{1/2}$

16) In Jack's class, 48 of the students are tall and 20 are short. In Michael's class 28 students are tall and 12 students are short. Which class has a higher ratio of tall to short students? $\underline{^{12}\!/_5}$ $\frac{48}{20},\ \frac{28}{12}$

17) The price of 6 apples at the Quick Market is \$1.52. The price of 5 of the same apples at Walmart is \$1.32. Which place is the better buy? $\underline{QM}$

18) The bakers at a Bakery can make 180 bagels in 6 hours. How many bagels can they bake in 16 hours? What is that rate per hour? $\underline{480, 30}$

19) You can buy 6 cans of green beans at a supermarket for \$3.48. How much does it cost to buy 38 cans of green beans? $\underline{22.04}$

Effortless Math Education

✍ Solve each proportion.

20) $\frac{3}{2} = \frac{9}{x} \Rightarrow x =$ ___6___

21) $\frac{7}{2} = \frac{x}{4} \Rightarrow x =$ ___14___

22) $\frac{1}{3} = \frac{2}{x} \Rightarrow x =$ ___6___

23) $\frac{1}{4} = \frac{5}{x} \Rightarrow x =$ ___20___

24) $\frac{9}{6} = \frac{x}{2} \Rightarrow x =$ ___3___

25) $\frac{3}{6} = \frac{5}{x} \Rightarrow x =$ ___10___

26) $\frac{7}{x} = \frac{2}{6} \Rightarrow x =$ ___21___

27) $\frac{2}{x} = \frac{4}{10} \Rightarrow x =$ ___5___

28) $\frac{3}{2} = \frac{x}{8} \Rightarrow x =$ ___12___

29) $\frac{x}{6} = \frac{5}{3} \Rightarrow x =$ ___10___

30) $\frac{3}{9} = \frac{5}{x} \Rightarrow x =$ ___15___

31) $\frac{4}{18} = \frac{2}{x} \Rightarrow x =$ ___9___

32) $\frac{6}{16} = \frac{3}{x} \Rightarrow x =$ ___8___

33) $\frac{2}{5} = \frac{x}{20} \Rightarrow x =$ ___8___

34) $\frac{28}{8} = \frac{x}{2} \Rightarrow x =$ ___7___

35) $\frac{3}{5} = \frac{x}{15} \Rightarrow x =$ ___9___

36) $\frac{2}{7} = \frac{x}{14} \Rightarrow x =$ ___4___

37) $\frac{x}{18} = \frac{3}{2} \Rightarrow x =$ ___27___

38) $\frac{x}{24} = \frac{2}{6} \Rightarrow x =$ ___8___

39) $\frac{5}{x} = \frac{4}{20} \Rightarrow x =$ ___25___

40) $\frac{10}{x} = \frac{20}{80} \Rightarrow x =$ ___40___

41) $\frac{90}{6} = \frac{x}{2} \Rightarrow x =$ ___30___

✍ Solve each problem.

42) Two rectangles are similar. The first is 8 *feet* wide and 32 *feet* long. The second is 12 *feet* wide. What is the length of the second rectangle?

___48___

43) Two rectangles are similar. One is 4.6 *meters* by 7 *meters*. The longer side of the second rectangle is 28 *meters*. What is the other side of the second rectangle? ___18.4___

$$\frac{6}{180} = \frac{16}{\alpha}$$

$$\frac{1.52}{6}$$

$$\frac{1.32}{5}$$

$$\frac{6}{3.48} = \frac{38}{}$$

**Effortless
Math
Education**

Chapter 4: Answers

1) $1:9$

2) $1:7$

3) $1:9$

4) $2:3$

5) $5:8$

6) $5:9$

7) $4:9$

8) $2:9$

9) $1:4$

10) $7:9$

11) $2:3$

12) $1:3$

13) $4:5$

14) 442

15) $1:2$

16) *Jack's class:* $\frac{48}{20} = \frac{12}{5}$ *Michael's class:* $\frac{28}{12} = \frac{7}{3}$ Jack's class has a higher ratio of tall to short student: $\frac{12}{5} > \frac{7}{3}$

17) Quick market

18) 480, 30 bagels per hour

19) $\$22.04$

20) 6

21) 14

22) 6

23) 20

24) 3

25) 10

26) 21

27) 5

28) 12

29) 10

30) 15

31) 9

32) 8

33) 8

34) 7

35) 9

36) 4

37) 27

38) 8

39) 25

40) 40

41) 30

42) 48 *feet*

43) 18.4 *meters*

Effortless Math Education

CHAPTER

5 Percentage

Math topics that you'll learn in this chapter:

- ☑ Percent Problems
- ☑ Percent of Increase and Decrease
- ☑ Discount, Tax and Tip
- ☑ Simple Interest

37

Percent Problems

- Percent is a ratio of a number and 100. It always has the same denominator, 100. The percent symbol is "%".

- Percent means "per 100". So, 20% is 20/100.

- In each percent problem, we are looking for the base, or part or the percent.

- Use these equations to find each missing section in a percent problem:

  ❖ Base = Part ÷ Percent

  ❖ Part = Percent × Base

  ❖ Percent = Part ÷ Base

Examples:

Example 1. What is 20% of 40?

Solution: In this problem, we have percent (20%) and base (40) and we are looking for the "part". Use this formula: $part = percent \times base$.

Then: $part = 20\% \times 40 = \frac{20}{100} \times 40 = 0.20 \times 40 = 8$. The answer: 20% of 40 is 8.

Example 2. 25 is what percent of 500?

Solution: In this problem, we are looking for the percent. Use this equation: $Percent = Part \div Base \rightarrow Percent = 25 \div 500 = 0.05 = 5\%$.

Then: 25 is 5 percent of 500.

Percent of Increase and Decrease

- Percent of change (increase or decrease) is a mathematical concept that represents the degree of change over time.

- To find the percentage of increase or decrease:

  1. New Number – Original Number

  2. The result ÷ Original Number × 100

- Or use this formula: Percent of change $= \frac{new\ number - original\ number}{original\ number} \times 100$

- Note: If your answer is a negative number, then this is a percentage decrease. If it is positive, then this is a percentage increase.

Examples:

Example 1. The price of a shirt increases from $30 to $40. What is the percentage increase?

Solution: First, find the difference: $40 - 30 = 10$

Then: $10 \div 30 \times 100 = \frac{10}{30} \times 100 = 33.33$. The percentage increase is 33.33. It means that the price of the shirt increased by 33.33%.

Example 2. The price of a table increased from $20 to $50. What is the percent of increase?

Solution: Use percentage formula:

$Percent\ of\ change = \frac{new\ number - original\ number}{original\ number} \times 100 =$

$\frac{50-20}{20} \times 100 = \frac{30}{20} \times 100 = 1.5 \times 100 = 150$. The percentage increase is 150. It means that the price of the table increased by 150%.

Discount, Tax and Tip

- To find the discount: Multiply the regular price by the rate of discount

- To find the selling price: Original price – discount

- To find tax: Multiply the tax rate to the taxable amount (income, property value, etc.)

- To find the tip, multiply the rate to the selling price.

Examples:

Example 1. With an 20% discount, Ella saved $50 on a dress. What was the original price of the dress?

Solution: let x be the original price of the dress. Then: $20 \% \; of \; x = 50$. Write an equation and solve for x: $0.20 \times x = 50 \rightarrow x = \frac{50}{0.20} = 250$. The original price of the dress was $250.

Example 2. Sophia purchased a new computer for a price of $820 at the Apple Store. What is the total amount her credit card is charged if the sales tax is 5%?

Solution: The taxable amount is $820, and the tax rate is 5%. Then: $Tax = 0.05 \times 820 = 41$
$Final \; price = Selling \; price + Tax \rightarrow final \; price = \$820 + \$41 = \$861$

Example 3. Nicole and her friends went out to eat at a restaurant. If their bill was $60.00 and they gave their server a 15% tip, how much did they pay altogether?

Solution: First, find the tip. To find the tip, multiply the rate to the bill amount. $Tip = 60 \times 0.15 = 9$. The final price is: $\$60 + \$9 = \$69$

bit.ly/2Je5lo0

Find more at

Simple Interest

- Simple Interest: The charge for borrowing money or the return for lending it.

- Simple interest is calculated on the initial amount (principal).

- To solve a simple interest problem, use this formula:

Interest = principal × rate × time $(I = p \times r \times t = prt)$

Examples:

Example 1. Find simple interest for $200 investment at 5% for 3 years.

Solution: Use Interest formula:
$I = prt$ ($P = \$200$, r $= 5\% = \frac{5}{100} = 0.05$ and $t = 3$)
Then: $I = 200 \times 0.05 \times 3 = \$30$

Example 2. Find simple interest for $1,200 at 8% for 6 years.

Solution: Use Interest formula:
$I = prt$ ($P = \$1,200$, r $= 8\% = \frac{8}{100} = 0.08$ and $t = 6$)
Then: $I = 1,200 \times 0.08 \times 6 = \$576$

Example 3. Andy received a student loan to pay for his educational expenses this year. What is the interest on the loan if he borrowed $4,500 at 6% for 5 years?

Solution: Use Interest formula: $I = prt$. $P = \$4,500$, r $= 6\% = 0.06$ and $t = 5$
Then: $I = 4,500 \times 0.06 \times 5 = \$1,350$

Example 4. Bob is starting his own small business. He borrowed $20,000 from the bank at a 8% rate for 6 months. Find the interest Bob will pay on this loan.

Solution: Use Interest formula:
$I = prt$. $P = \$20,000$, r $= 8\% = 0.08$ and $t = 0.5$ (6 months is half year).
Then: $I = 20,000 \times 0.08 \times 0.5 = \$800$

bit.ly/3nJli3D

Find more at

Chapter 5: Practices

✍ Solve each problem.

1) What is 15% of 60? __9__

2) What is 55% of 800? __440__

3) What is 22% of 120? __26.4__

4) What is 18% of 40? __7.2__

5) 90 is what percent of 200? __45__ %

6) 30 is what percent of 150? __20__ %

7) 14 is what percent of 250? __5.6__ %

8) 60 is what percent of 300? __20__ %

9) 30 is 120 percent of what number? __25__

10) 120 is 20 percent of what number? __600__

11) 15 is 5 percent of what number? __300__

12) 22 is 20% of what number? __110__

✍ Solve each problem.

13) Bob got a raise, and his hourly wage increased from $15 to $21. What is the percent increase? __40__ %

14) The price of a pair of shoes increases from $32 to $36. What is the percent increase? __12.5__ %

15) At a Coffee Shop, the price of a cup of coffee increased from $1.35 to $1.62. What is the percent increase in the cost of the coffee? __20__ %

16) A $45 shirt now selling for $36 is discounted by what percent? __20__ %

17) Joe scored 30 out of 35 marks in Algebra, 20 out of 30 marks in science and 58 out of 70 marks in mathematics. In which subject his percentage of marks is best? __ALGEBRA__

18) Emma purchased a computer for $420. The computer is regularly priced at $480. What was the percent discount Emma received on the computer? __12.5__

19) A chemical solution contains 15% alcohol. If there is 54 ml of alcohol, what is the volume of the solution? __360__

Find the selling price of each item.

20) Original price of a computer: $600

    Tax: 8%, Selling price: $ _648_

21) Original price of a laptop: $450

    Tax: 10%, Selling price: $ _495_

22) Nicolas hired a moving company. The company charged $500 for its services, and Nicolas gives the movers a 14% tip. How much does Nicolas tip the movers? $ _70_

23) Mason has lunch at a restaurant and the cost of his meal is $40. Mason wants to leave a 20% tip. What is Mason's total bill, including tip?
    $ _48_

Determine the simple interest for the following loans.

24) $1,000 *at* 5% *for* 4 *years.* $ _200_

25) $400 *at* 3% *for* 5 *years.* $ _60_

26) $240 *at* 4% *for* 3 *years.* $ _288_

27) $500 *at* 4.5% *for* 6 years. $ _135_

Solve.

28) A new car, valued at $20,000, depreciates at 8% per year. What is the value of the car one year after purchase? $ _18,400_

29) Sara puts $7,000 into an investment yielding 3% annual simple interest; she left the money in for five years. How much interest does Sara get at the end of those five years? $ _1,050_

Effortless

Math

Education

Chapter 5: Answers

1)	9	16)	20%
2)	440	17)	Algebra
3)	26.4	18)	12.5%
4)	7.2	19)	360 ml
5)	45%	20)	$648.00
6)	20%	21)	$495.00
7)	5.6%	22)	$70.00
8)	20%	23)	$48.00
9)	25	24)	$200.00
10)	600	25)	$60.00
11)	300	26)	$28.80
12)	110	27)	$135.00
13)	40%	28)	$18.400
14)	12.5%	29)	$1,050
15)	20%		

CHAPTER

6 Exponents and Variables

Math topics that you'll learn in this chapter:

☑ Multiplication Property of Exponents

☑ Division Property of Exponents

☑ Powers of Products and Quotients

☑ Zero and Negative Exponents

☑ Negative Exponents and Negative Bases

☑ Scientific Notation

☑ Radicals

45

Multiplication Property of Exponents

- Exponents are shorthand for repeated multiplication of the same number by itself. For example, instead of 2×2, we can write 2^2. For $3 \times 3 \times 3 \times 3$, we can write 3^4

- In algebra, a variable is a letter used to stand for a number. The most common letters are: $x, y, z, a, b, c, m,$ and n.

- Exponent's rules: $x^a \times x^b = x^{a+b}$, $\frac{x^a}{x^b} = x^{a-b}$

$$(x^a)^b = x^{a \times b} \qquad\qquad (xy)^a = x^a \times y^a \qquad\qquad \left(\frac{a}{b}\right)^c = \frac{a^c}{b^c}$$

Examples:

Example 1. Multiply. $2x^2 \times 3x^4$

Solution: Use Exponent's rules: $x^a \times x^b = x^{a+b} \rightarrow x^2 \times x^4 = x^{2+4} = x^6$
Then: $2x^2 \times 3x^4 = 6x^6$

Example 2. Simplify. $(x^4 y^2)^2$

Solution: Use Exponent's rules: $(x^a)^b = x^{a \times b}$.
Then: $(x^4 y^2)^2 = x^{4 \times 2} y^{2 \times 2} = x^8 y^4$

Example 3. Multiply. $5x^8 \times 6x^5$

Solution: Use Exponent's rules: $x^a \times x^b = x^{a+b} \rightarrow x^8 \times x^5 = x^{8+5} = x^{13}$
Then: $5x^8 \times 6x^5 = 30x^{13}$

Example 4. Simplify. $(x^4 y^7)^3$

Solution: Use Exponent's rules: $(x^a)^b = x^{a \times b}$.
Then: $(x^4 y^7)^3 = x^{4 \times 3} y^{7 \times 3} = x^{12} y^{21}$

Division Property of Exponents

- Exponents are shorthand for repeated multiplication of the same number by itself. For example, instead of 3×3, we can write 3^2. For $2 \times 2 \times 2$, we can write 2^3

- For division of exponents use following formulas:

$$\frac{x^a}{x^b} = x^{a-b} \ , \ x \neq 0, \quad \frac{x^a}{x^b} = \frac{1}{x^{b-a}} \ , \ x \neq 0, \qquad \frac{1}{x^b} = x^{-b}$$

Examples:

Example 1. Simplify. $\frac{16x^3 y}{2xy^2} =$

Solution: First, cancel the common factor: $2 \rightarrow \frac{16x^3 y}{2xy^2} = \frac{8x^3 y}{xy^2}$

Use Exponent's rules: $\frac{x^a}{x^b} = x^{a-b} \ \rightarrow \frac{x^3}{x} = x^{3-1} = x^2$ and $\frac{y}{y^2} = \frac{1}{y^{2-1}} = \frac{1}{y}$

Then: $\frac{16x^3 y}{2xy^2} = \frac{8x^2}{y}$

Example 2. Simplify. $\frac{24x^8}{3x^6} =$

Solution: Use Exponent's rules: $\frac{x^a}{x^b} = x^{b-a} \ \rightarrow \frac{x^8}{x^6} = x^{8-6} = x^2$

Then: $\frac{24x^8}{3x^6} = 8x^2$

Example 3. Simplify. $\frac{7x^4 y^2}{28x^3 y} =$

Solution: First, cancel the common factor: $7 \rightarrow \frac{x^4 y^2}{4x^3 y}$

Use Exponent's rules: $\frac{x^a}{x^b} = x^{a-b} \ \rightarrow \frac{x^4}{x^3} = x^{4-3} = x$ and $\frac{y^2}{y} = y$

Then: $\frac{7x^4 y^2}{28x^3 y} = \frac{xy}{4}$

Powers of Products and Quotients

- Exponents are shorthand for repeated multiplication of the same number by itself. For example, instead of $2 \times 2 \times 2$, we can write 2^3. For $3 \times 3 \times 3 \times 3$, we can write 3^4

- For any nonzero numbers a and b and any integer x, $(ab)^x = a^x \times b^x$ and $\left(\frac{a}{b}\right)^c = \frac{a^c}{b^c}$

Examples:

Example 1. Simplify. $(3x^3y^2)^2$

Solution: Use Exponent's rules: $(x^a)^b = x^{a \times b}$
$(3x^3y^2)^2 = (3)^2(x^3)^2(y^2)^2 = 9x^{3 \times 2}y^{2 \times 2} = 9x^6y^4$

Example 2. Simplify. $\left(\frac{2x^3}{3x^2}\right)^2$

Solution: First, cancel the common factor: $x \rightarrow \left(\frac{2x^3}{3x^2}\right) = \left(\frac{2x}{3}\right)^2$
Use Exponent's rules: $\left(\frac{a}{b}\right)^c = \frac{a^c}{b^c}$, Then: $\left(\frac{2x}{3}\right)^2 = \frac{(2x)^2}{(3)^2} = \frac{4x^2}{9}$

Example 3. Simplify. $\left(-4x^3y^5\right)^2$

Solution: Use Exponent's rules: $(x^a)^b = x^{a \times b}$
$$\left(-4x^3y^5\right)^2 = (-4)^2(x^3)^2\left(y^5\right)^2 = 16x^{3 \times 2}y^{5 \times 2} = 16x^6y^{10}$$

Example 4. Simplify. $\left(\frac{5x}{4x^2}\right)^2$

Solution: First, cancel the common factor: $x \rightarrow \left(\frac{5x}{4x^2}\right)^2 = \left(\frac{5}{4x}\right)^2$
Use Exponent's rules: $\left(\frac{a}{b}\right)^c = \frac{a^c}{b^c}$, Then: $\left(\frac{5}{4x}\right)^2 = \frac{5^2}{(4x)^2} = \frac{25}{16x^2}$

Zero and Negative Exponents

- Zero-Exponent Rule: $a^0 = 1$, this means that anything raised to the zero power is 1. For example: $(5xy)^0 = 1$

- A negative exponent simply means that the base is on the wrong side of the fraction line, so you need to flip the base to the other side. For instance, "x^{-2}" (pronounced as "ecks to the minus two") just means "x^2" but underneath, as in $\frac{1}{x^2}$.

Examples:

Example 1. Evaluate. $\left(\frac{4}{5}\right)^{-2} =$

Solution: Use negative exponent's rule: $\left(\frac{x^a}{x^b}\right)^{-2} = \left(\frac{x^b}{x^a}\right)^2 \rightarrow \left(\frac{4}{5}\right)^{-2} = \left(\frac{5}{4}\right)^2 =$
Then: $\left(\frac{5}{4}\right)^2 = \frac{5^2}{4^2} = \frac{25}{16}$

Example 2. Evaluate. $\left(\frac{3}{2}\right)^{-3} =$

Solution: Use negative exponent's rule: $\left(\frac{x^a}{x^b}\right)^{-3} = \left(\frac{x^b}{x^a}\right)^3 \rightarrow \left(\frac{3}{2}\right)^{-3} = \left(\frac{2}{3}\right)^3 =$
Then: $\left(\frac{2}{3}\right)^3 = \frac{2^3}{3^3} = \frac{8}{27}$

Example 3. Evaluate. $\left(\frac{a}{b}\right)^0 =$

Solution: Use zero-exponent Rule: $a^0 = 1$

Then: $\left(\frac{a}{b}\right)^0 = 1$

Example 4. Evaluate. $\left(\frac{4}{7}\right)^{-1} =$

Solution: Use negative exponent's rule: $\left(\frac{x^a}{x^b}\right)^{-1} = \left(\frac{x^b}{x^a}\right)^1 \rightarrow \left(\frac{4}{7}\right)^{-1} = \left(\frac{7}{4}\right)^1 = \frac{7}{4}$

bit.ly/3rnkh4v

Find more at

Negative Exponents and Negative Bases

- A negative exponent is the reciprocal of that number with a positive exponent. $(3)^{-2} = \frac{1}{3^2}$

- To simplify a negative exponent, make the power positive!

- The parenthesis is important! -5^{-2} is not the same as $(-5)^{-2}$

$$-5^{-2} = -\frac{1}{5^2} \text{ and } (-5)^{-2} = +\frac{1}{5^2}$$

Examples:

Example 1. Simplify. $\left(\frac{2a}{3c}\right)^{-2} =$

Solution: Use negative exponent's rule: $\left(\frac{x^a}{x^b}\right)^{-2} = \left(\frac{x^b}{x^a}\right)^2 \rightarrow \left(\frac{2a}{3c}\right)^{-2} = \left(\frac{3c}{2a}\right)^2$

Now use exponent's rule: $\left(\frac{a}{b}\right)^c = \frac{a^c}{b^c} \rightarrow = \left(\frac{3c}{2a}\right)^2 = \frac{3^2c^2}{2^2a^2}$

Then: $\frac{3^2c^2}{2^2a^2} = \frac{9c^2}{4a^2}$

Example 2. Simplify. $\left(\frac{x}{4y}\right)^{-3} =$

Solution: Use negative exponent's rule: $\left(\frac{x^a}{x^b}\right)^{-3} = \left(\frac{x^b}{x^a}\right)^3 \rightarrow \left(\frac{x}{4y}\right)^{-3} = \left(\frac{4y}{x}\right)^3$

Now use exponent's rule: $\left(\frac{a}{b}\right)^c = \frac{a^c}{b^c} \rightarrow \left(\frac{4y}{x}\right)^3 = \frac{4^3y^3}{x^3} = \frac{64y^3}{x^3}$

Example 3. Simplify. $\left(\frac{5a}{2c}\right)^{-2} =$

Solution: Use negative exponent's rule: $\left(\frac{x^a}{x^b}\right)^{-2} = \left(\frac{x^b}{x^a}\right)^2 \rightarrow \left(\frac{5a}{2c}\right)^{-2} = \left(\frac{2c}{5a}\right)^2$

Now use exponent's rule: $\left(\frac{a}{b}\right)^c = \frac{a^c}{b^c} \rightarrow = \left(\frac{2c}{5a}\right)^2 = \frac{2^2c^2}{5^2a^2}$

Then: $\frac{2^2c^2}{5^2a^2} = \frac{4c^2}{25a^2}$

bit.ly/3nPROSM
Find more at

EffortlessMath.com

Scientific Notation

- Scientific notation is used to write very big or very small numbers in decimal form.

- In scientific notation, all numbers are written in the form of: $m \times 10^n$, where m is greater than 1 and less than 10.

- To convert a number from scientific notation to standard form, move the decimal point to the left (if the exponent of ten is a negative number), or to the right (if the exponent is positive).

Examples:

Example 1. Write 0.00024 in scientific notation.

Solution: First, move the decimal point to the right so you have a number between 1 and 10. That number is 2.4. Now, determine how many places the decimal moved in step 1 by the power of 10. We moved the decimal point 4 digits to the right. Then: $10^{-4} \rightarrow$ When the decimal moved to the right, the exponent is negative. Then: $0.00024 = 2.4 \times 10^{-4}$

Example 2. Write 3.8×10^{-5} in standard notation.

Solution: $10^{-5} \rightarrow$ When the decimal moved to the right, the exponent is negative. Then: $3.8 \times 10^{-5} = 0.000038$

Example 3. Write 0.00031 in scientific notation.

Solution: First, move the decimal point to the right so you have a number between 1 and 10. Then: $m = 3.1$, Now, determine how many places the decimal moved in step 1 by the power of 10. $10^{-4} \rightarrow$ Then: $0.00031 = 3.1 \times 10^{-4}$

Example 4. Write 6.2×10^5 in standard notation.

Solution: $10^5 \rightarrow$ The exponent is positive 5. Then, move the decimal point to the right five digits. (remember 6.2 = 6.20000), Then: $6.2 \times 10^5 = 620,000$

bit.ly/3nOwJYP

Find more at

Radicals

- If n is a positive integer and x is a real number, then: $\sqrt[n]{x} = x^{\frac{1}{n}}$,

$$\sqrt[n]{xy} = x^{\frac{1}{n}} \times y^{\frac{1}{n}}, \ \sqrt[n]{\frac{x}{y}} = \frac{x^{\frac{1}{n}}}{y^{\frac{1}{n}}}, \text{ and } \sqrt[n]{x} \times \sqrt[n]{y} = \sqrt[n]{xy}$$

- A square root of x is a number r whose square is: $r^2 = x$ (r is a square root of x)

- To add and subtract radicals, we need to have the same values under the radical. For example: $\sqrt{3} + \sqrt{3} = 2\sqrt{3}, \ 3\sqrt{5} - \sqrt{5} = 2\sqrt{5}$

Examples:

Example 1. Find the square root of $\sqrt{121}$.

Solution: First, factor the number: $121 = 11^2$, Then: $\sqrt{121} = \sqrt{11^2}$, Now use radical rule: $\sqrt[n]{a^n} = a$. Then: $\sqrt{121} = \sqrt{11^2} = 11$

Example 2. Evaluate. $\sqrt{4} \times \sqrt{16} =$

Solution: Find the values of $\sqrt{4}$ and $\sqrt{16}$. Then: $\sqrt{4} \times \sqrt{16} = 2 \times 4 = 8$

Example 3. Solve. $5\sqrt{2} + 9\sqrt{2}$.

Solution: Since we have the same values under the radical, we can add these two radicals: $5\sqrt{2} + 9\sqrt{2} = 14\sqrt{2}$

Example 4. Evaluate. $\sqrt{2} \times \sqrt{50} =$

Solution: Use this radical rule: $\sqrt[n]{x} \times \sqrt[n]{y} = \sqrt[n]{xy} \rightarrow \sqrt{2} \times \sqrt{50} = \sqrt{100}$
The square root of 100 is 10. Then: $\sqrt{2} \times \sqrt{50} = \sqrt{100} = 10$

bit.ly/2WEATqr

Find more at

Chapter 6: Practices

✎ Find the products.

1) $x^2 \times 4xy^2 =$ $4x^3y^2$

2) $3x^2y \times 5x^3y^2 =$ $15x^5y^3$

3) $6x^4y^2 \times x^2y^3 =$ $6x^2y^5$

4) $7xy^3 \times 2x^2y =$ $14x^3y^4$

5) $-5x^5y^5 \times x^3y^2 =$ $-5x^8y^7$

6) $-8x^3y^2 \times 3x^3y^2 =$ $-24x^6y^4$

7) $-6x^2y^6 \times 5x^4y^2 =$ $-30x^6y^8$

8) $-3x^3y^3 \times 2x^3y^2 =$ $-6x^4y^5$

9) $-6x^5y^3 \times 4x^4y^3 =$ $-24x^9y^6$

10) $-2x^4y^3 \times 5x^6y^2 =$ $-10x^{10}y^5$

11) $-7y^6 \times 3x^6y^3 =$ $-21x^6y^9$

12) $-9x^4 \times 2x^4y^2 =$ $-18x^8y^2$

✎ Simplify.

13) $\frac{5^3 \times 5^4}{5^9 \times 5} =$ $\frac{5^7}{5^{10}} = \frac{1}{125}$

14) $\frac{3^3 \times 3^2}{7^2 \times 7} =$ $\frac{3^5}{7^3} = \frac{243}{343}$

15) $\frac{15x^5y^2}{5x^3} =$ $3x^2$

16) $\frac{16x^3}{4x^5} =$

17) $\frac{72y^2}{8x^3y^6} =$

18) $\frac{10x^3y^4}{50x^2y^3} =$

19) $\frac{13y^2}{52x^4y^4} =$

20) $\frac{50xy^3}{200x^3y^4} =$

21) $\frac{48x^2}{56x^2y^2} =$

22) $\frac{81y^6x}{54x^4y^3} =$

✎ Solve.

23) $(x^3y^3)^2 =$

24) $(3x^3y^4)^3 =$

25) $(4x \times 6xy^3)^2 =$

26) $(5x \times 2y^3)^3 =$

27) $\left(\frac{9x}{x^3}\right)^2 =$

28) $(\frac{3y}{18y^2})^2 =$

29) $\left(\frac{3x^2y^3}{24x^4y^2}\right)^3 =$

30) $\left(\frac{26x^5y^3}{52x^3y^5}\right)^2 =$

31) $\left(\frac{18x^7y^4}{72x^5y^2}\right)^2 =$

32) $\left(\frac{12x^6y^4}{48x^5y^3}\right)^2 =$

Effortless Math Education

✍ **Evaluate each expression. (Zero and Negative Exponents)**

33) $\left(\frac{1}{4}\right)^{-2} =$

34) $\left(\frac{1}{3}\right)^{-2} =$

35) $\left(\frac{1}{7}\right)^{-3} =$

36) $\left(\frac{2}{5}\right)^{-3} =$

37) $\left(\frac{2}{3}\right)^{-3} =$

38) $\left(\frac{3}{5}\right)^{-4} =$

✍ **Write each expression with positive exponents.**

39) $x^{-7} =$

40) $3y^{-5} =$

41) $15y^{-3} =$

42) $-20x^{-4} =$

43) $12a^{-3}b^5 =$

44) $25a^3b^{-4}c^{-3} =$

45) $-4x^5y^{-3}z^{-6} =$

46) $\frac{18y}{x^3y^{-2}} =$

47) $\frac{20a^{-2}b}{-12c^{-4}}$

✍ **Write each number in scientific notation.**

48) $0.00412 =$

49) $0.000053 =$

50) $66{,}000 =$

51) $72{,}000{,}000 =$

✍ **Evaluate.**

52) $\sqrt{8} \times \sqrt{8} =$..............

53) $\sqrt{36} - \sqrt{9} =$............

54) $\sqrt{81} + \sqrt{16} =$

55) $\sqrt{4} \times \sqrt{25} =$............

56) $\sqrt{2} \times \sqrt{32} =$............

57) $4\sqrt{3} + 5\sqrt{3} =$...........

Effortless Math Education

Effortless
Math
Education

Chapter 6: Answers

1) $4x^3y^2$

2) $15x^5y^3$

3) $6x^6y^5$

4) $14x^3y^4$

5) $-5x^8y^7$

6) $-24x^6y^4$

7) $-30x^6y^8$

8) $-6x^6y^5$

9) $-24x^9y^6$

10) $-10x^{10}y^5$

11) $-21x^6y^9$

12) $-18x^8y^2$

13) $\dfrac{1}{125}$

14) $\dfrac{243}{343}$

15) $3x^2$

16) $\dfrac{4}{x^2}$

17) $\dfrac{9}{x^3y^4}$

18) $\dfrac{xy}{5}$

19) $\dfrac{1}{4x^4y^2}$

20) $\dfrac{1}{4x^2y}$

21) $\dfrac{6}{7y^2}$

22) $\dfrac{3y^3}{2x^3}$

23) x^6y^6

24) $27x^9y^{12}$

25) $576x^4y^6$

26) $1,000x^3y^9$

27) $\dfrac{81}{x^4}$

28) $\dfrac{1}{36y^2}$

29) $\dfrac{y^3}{512x^6}$

30) $\dfrac{x^4}{4y^4}$

31) $\dfrac{x^4y^4}{16}$

32) $\dfrac{x^2y^2}{16}$

33) 16

34) 9

35) 343

36) $\dfrac{125}{8}$

37) $\dfrac{27}{8}$

38) $\dfrac{625}{81}$

39) $\dfrac{1}{x^7}$

40) $\dfrac{3}{y^5}$

41) $\dfrac{15}{y^3}$

42) $-\dfrac{20}{x^4}$

43) $\dfrac{12b^5}{a^3}$

44) $\dfrac{25a^3}{b^4c^3}$

45) $-\dfrac{4x^5}{y^3z^6}$

46) $\dfrac{18y^3}{x^3}$

47) $-\dfrac{5bc^4}{3a^2}$

48) 4.12×10^{-3}

49) 5.3×10^{-5}

50) 6.6×10^4

51) 7.2×10^7

52) 8

53) 3

54) 13

55) 10

56) 8

57) $9\sqrt{3}$

CHAPTER

7 Expressions and Variables

Math topics that you'll learn in this chapter:

- ☑ Simplifying Variable Expressions
- ☑ Simplifying Polynomial Expressions
- ☑ The Distributive Property
- ☑ Evaluating One Variable
- ☑ Evaluating Two Variables

57

Simplifying Variable Expressions

- In algebra, a variable is a letter used to stand for a number. The most common letters are $x, y, z, a, b, c, m,$ and n.

- An algebraic expression is an expression that contains integers, variables, and math operations such as addition, subtraction, multiplication, division, etc.

- In an expression, we can combine "like" terms. (values with same variable and same power)

Examples:

Example 1. Simplify. $(4x + 2x + 4) =$

Solution: In this expression, there are three terms: $4x, 2x,$ and 4. Two terms are "like terms": $4x$ and $2x$. Combine like terms. $4x + 2x = 6x$. Then: $(4x + 2x + 4) = 6x + 4$ (***remember you cannot combine variables and numbers.***)

Example 2. Simplify. $-2x^2 - 5x + 4x^2 - 9 =$

Solution: Combine "like" terms: $-2x^2 + 4x^2 = 2x^2$.
Then: $-2x^2 - 5x + 4x^2 - 9 = 2x^2 - 5x - 9$.

Example 3. Simplify. $(-8 + 6x^2 + 3x^2 + 9x) =$

Solution: Combine like terms. Then:
$(-8 + 6x^2 + 3x^2 + 9x) = 9x^2 + 9x - 8$

Example 4. Simplify. $-10x + 6x^2 - 3x + 9x^2 =$

Solution: Combine "like" terms: $-10x - 3x = -13x$, and $6x^2 + 9x^2 = 15x^2$
Then: $-10x + 6x^2 - 3x + 9x^2 = -13x + 15x^2$. Write in standard form (biggest powers first): $-13x + 15x^2 = 15x^2 - 13x$

Simplifying Polynomial Expressions

- In mathematics, a polynomial is an expression consisting of variables and coefficients that involves only the operations of addition, subtraction, multiplication, and non–negative integer exponents of variables. $P(x) = a_n x^n + a_{n-1} x^{n-1} + \dots + a_2 x^2 + a_1 x + a_0$

- Polynomials must always be simplified as much as possible. It means you must add together any like terms. (values with same variable and same power)

Examples:

Example 1. Simplify this Polynomial Expressions. $3x^2 - 6x^3 - 2x^3 + 4x^4$

Solution: Combine "like" terms: $-6x^3 - 2x^3 = -8x^3$
Then: $3x^2 - 6x^3 - 2x^3 + 4x^4 = 3x^2 - 8x^3 + 4x^4$
Now, write the expression in standard form: $4x^4 - 8x^3 + 3x^2$

Example 2. Simplify this expression. $(-5x^2 + 2x^3) - (3x^3 - 6x^2) =$

Solution: First, use distributive property: $\rightarrow$ multiply $(-)$ into $(3x^3 - 6x^2)$
$(-5x^2 + 2x^3) - (3x^3 - 6x^2) = -5x^2 + 2x^3 - 3x^3 + 6x^2$
Then combine "like" terms: $-5x^2 + 2x^3 - 3x^3 + 6x^2 = x^2 - x^3$
And write in standard form: $x^2 - x^3 = -x^3 + x^2$

Example 3. Simplify. $3x^3 - 9x^4 - 8x^2 + 12x^4 =$

Solution: Combine "like" terms:
$-9x^4 + 12x^4 = 3x^4$
Then: $3x^3 - 9x^4 - 8x^2 + 12x^4 = 3x^3 + 3x^4 - 8x^2$
And write in standard form: $3x^3 + 3x^4 - 8x^2 = 3x^4 + 3x^3 - 8x^2$

bit.ly/2WT5gtn

Find more at

The Distributive Property

- The distributive property (or the distributive property of multiplication over addition and subtraction) simplifies and solves expressions in the form of: $a(b + c)$ or $a(b - c)$

- The distributive property is multiplying a term outside the parentheses by the terms inside.

- Distributive Property rule: $a(b + c) = ab + ac$

Examples:

Example 1. Simply using the distributive property. $(-2)(x + 3)$

Solution: Use Distributive Property rule: $a(b + c) = ab + ac$
$(-2)(x + 3) = (-2 \times x) + (-2) \times (3) = -2x - 6$

Example 2. Simply. $(-5)(-2x - 6)$

Solution: Use Distributive Property rule: $a(b + c) = ab + ac$
$(-5)(-2x - 6) = (-5 \times -2x) + (-5) \times (-6) = 10x + 30$

Example 3. Simply. $(7)(2x - 8) - 12x$

Solution: First, simplify $(7)(2x - 8)$ using the distributive property.
Then: $(7)(2x - 8) = 14x - 56$
Now combine like terms: $(7)(2x - 8) - 12x = 14x - 56 - 12x$
In this expression, $14x$ and $-12x$ are "like terms" and we can combine them.
$14x - 12x = 2x$. Then: $14x - 56 - 12x = 2x - 56$

bit.ly/38qCaXs
Find more at

Evaluating One Variable

- To evaluate one variable expression, find the variable and substitute a number for that variable.

- Perform the arithmetic operations.

Examples:

Example 1. Calculate this expression for $x = 2$. $8 + 2x$

Solution: First, substitute 2 for x

Then: $8 + 2x = 8 + 2(2)$

Now, use order of operation to find the answer: $8 + 2(2) = 8 + 4 = 12$

Example 2. Evaluate this expression for $x = -1$. $4x - 8$

Solution: First, substitute -1 for x,

Then: $4x - 8 = 4(-1) - 8$

Now, use order of operation to find the answer: $4(-1) - 8 = -4 - 8 = -12$

Example 3. Find the value of this expression when $x = 4$. $16 - 5x$

Solution: First, substitute 4 for x,

Then: $16 - 5x = 16 - 5(4) = 16 - 20 = -4$

Example 4. Solve this expression for $x = -3$. $15 + 7x$

Solution: Substitute -3 for x,

Then: $15 + 7x = 15 + 7(-3) = 15 - 21 = -6$

Evaluating Two Variables

- To evaluate an algebraic expression, substitute a number for each variable.

- Perform the arithmetic operations to find the value of the expression.

Examples:

Example 1. Calculate this expression for $a = 2$ and $b = -1$. $4a - 3b$

Solution: First, substitute 2 for a, and -1 for b ,
Then: $4a - 3b = 4(2) - 3(-1)$
Now, use order of operation to find the answer: $4(2) - 3(-1) = 8 + 3 = 11$

Example 2. Evaluate this expression for $x = -2$ and $y = 2$. $3x + 6y$

Solution: Substitute -2 for x, and 2 for y ,
Then: $3x + 6y = 3(-2) + 6(2) = -6 + 12 = 6$

Example 3. Find the value of this expression $2(6a - 5b)$ when $a = -1$ and $b = 4$.

Solution: Substitute -1 for a, and 4 for b ,
Then: $2(6a - 5b) = 12a - 10b = 12(-1) - 10(4) = -12 - 40 = -52$

Example 4. Solve this expression. $-7x - 2y$, $x = 4$, $y = -3$

Solution: Substitute 4 for x, and -3 for y and simplify.
Then: $-7x - 2y = -7(4) - 2(-3) = -28 + 6 = -22$

Chapter 7: Practices

✍ **Simplify each expression.**

1) $(3 + 4x - 1) =$

2) $(-5 - 2x + 7) =$

3) $(12x - 5x - 4) =$

4) $(-16x + 24x - 9) =$

5) $(6x + 5 - 15x) =$

6) $2 + 5x - 8x - 6 =$

7) $5x + 10 - 3x - 22 =$

8) $-5 - 3x^2 - 6 + 4x =$

9) $-6 + 9x^2 - 3 + x =$

10) $5x^2 + 3x - 10x - 3 =$

11) $4x^2 - 2x - 6x + 5 - 8 =$

12) $3x^2 - 5x - 7x + 2 - 4 =$

13) $9x^2 - x - 5x + 3 - 9 =$

14) $2x^2 - 7x - 3x^2 + 4x + 6 =$

✍ **Simplify each polynomial.**

15) $5x^2 + 3x^3 - 9x^2 + 2x =$ ....

16) $8x^4 + 2x^5 - 7x^4 + 3x^2 =$ ....

17) $15x^3 + 11x - 5x^2 - 9x^3 =$ ....

18) $(7x^3 - 3x^2) + (5x^2 - 13x) =$ ....

19) $(12x^4 + 6x^3) + (x^3 - 5x^4) =$ ....

20) $(15x^5 - 8x^3) - (4x^3 + x^2) =$ ....

21) $(14x^4 + 7x^3) - (x^3 - 24) =$ ....

22) $(20x^4 + 6x^3) - (-x^3 - 2x^4) =$ ....

23) $(x^2 + 9x^3) + (-22x^2 + 6x^3) =$ ....

24) $(4x^4 - 2x^3) + (-5x^3 - 8x^4) =$ ....

Effortless
Math
Education

✎ **Use the distributive property to simply each expression.**

25) $2(6 + x) =$ _____   30) $(-1)(-9 + x) =$ _____

26) $5(3 - 2x) =$ _____   31) $(-6)(3x - 2) =$ _____

27) $7(1 - 5x) =$ _____   32) $(-x + 12)(-4) =$ _____

28) $(3 - 4x)7 =$ _____   33) $(-2)(1 - 6x) =$ _____

29) $6(2 - 3x) =$ _____   34) $(-5x - 3)(-8) =$ _____

✎ **Evaluate each expression using the value given.**

35) $x = 4 \rightarrow 10 - x =$ ____   42) $x = -6 \rightarrow 5 - x =$ ____

36) $x = 6 \rightarrow x + 8 =$ ____   43) $x = -3 \rightarrow 22 - 3x =$ ____

37) $x = 3 \rightarrow 2x - 6 =$ ____   44) $x = -7 \rightarrow 10 - 9x =$ ____

38) $x = 2 \rightarrow 10 - 4x =$ ____   45) $x = -10 \rightarrow 40 - 3x =$ ____

39) $x = 7 \rightarrow 8x - 3 =$ ____   46) $x = -2 \rightarrow 20x - 5 =$ ____

40) $x = 9 \rightarrow 20 - 2x =$ ____   47) $x = -5 \rightarrow -10x - 8 =$ ___

41) $x = 5 \rightarrow 10x - 30 =$ ___   48) $x = -4 \rightarrow -1 - 4x =$ ___

✎ **Evaluate each expression using the values given.**

49) $x = 2, y = 1 \rightarrow 2x + 7y =$ _____

50) $a = 3, b = 5 \rightarrow 3a - 5b =$ _____

51) $x = 6, y = 2 \rightarrow 3x - 2y + 8 =$ _____

52) $a = -2, b = 3 \rightarrow -5a + 2b + 6 =$ _____

53) $x = -4, y = -3 \rightarrow -4x + 10 - 8y =$ _____

Chapter 7: Answers

1) $4x + 2$

2) $-2x + 2$

3) $7x - 4$

4) $8x - 9$

5) $-9x + 5$

6) $-3x - 4$

7) $2x - 12$

8) $-3x^2 + 4x - 11$

9) $9x^2 + x - 9$

10) $5x^2 - 7x - 3$

11) $4x^2 - 8x - 3$

12) $3x^2 - 12x - 2$

13) $9x^2 - 6x - 6$

14) $-x^2 - 3x + 6$

15) $3x^3 - 4x^2 + 2x$

16) $2x^5 + x^4 + 3x^2$

17) $6x^3 - 5x^2 + 11x$

18) $7x^3 + 2x^2 - 13x$

19) $7x^4 + 7x^3$

20) $15x^5 - 12x^3 - x^2$

21) $14x^4 + 6x^3 + 24$

22) $22x^4 + 7x^3$

23) $15x^3 - 21x^2$

24) $-4x^4 - 7x^3$

25) $2x + 12$

26) $-10x + 15$

27) $-35x + 7$

28) $-28x + 21$

29) $-18x + 12$

30) $-x + 9$

31) $-18x + 12$

32) $4x - 48$

33) $12x - 2$

34) $40x + 24$

35) 6

36) 14

37) 0

38) 2

39) 53

40) 2

41) 20

42) 11

43) 31

44) 73

45) 70

46) -45

47) 42

48) 15

49) 11

50) -16

51) 22

52) 22

53) 50

8 Equations and Inequalities

Math topics that you'll learn in this chapter:

- ☑ One-Step Equations
- ☑ Multi-Step Equations
- ☑ System of Equations
- ☑ Graphing Single–Variable Inequalities
- ☑ One-Step Inequalities
- ☑ Multi-Step Inequalities

67

One–Step Equations

- The values of two expressions on both sides of an equation are equal. Example: $ax = b$. In this equation, ax is equal to b.

- Solving an equation means finding the value of the variable.

- You only need to perform one Math operation to solve the one-step equations.

- To solve a one-step equation, find the inverse (opposite) operation is being performed.

- The inverse operations are:

  ❖ Addition and subtraction
  ❖ Multiplication and division

Examples:

Example 1. Solve this equation for x. $4x = 16, x = ?$

Solution: Here, the operation is multiplication (variable x is multiplied by 4) and its inverse operation is division. To solve this equation, divide both sides of equation by 4: $4x = 16 \rightarrow \frac{4x}{4} = \frac{16}{4} \rightarrow x = 4$

Example 2. Solve this equation. $x + 8 = 0$, $x = ?$

Solution: In this equation 8 is added to the variable x. The inverse operation of addition is subtraction. To solve this equation, subtract 8 from both sides of the equation: $x + 8 - 8 = 0 - 8$. Then: $\rightarrow x = -8$

Example 3. Solve this equation for x. $x + 12 = 0$

Solution: Here, the operation is addition and its inverse operation is subtraction. To solve this equation, subtract 12 from both sides of the equation:
$$x + 12 - 12 = 0 - 12 \rightarrow x = -12$$

bit.ly/37Jq0tK
Find more at

Multi–Step Equations

- To solve a multi-step equation, combine "like" terms on one side.

- Bring variables to one side by adding or subtracting.

- Simplify using the inverse of addition or subtraction.

- Simplify further by using the inverse of multiplication or division.

- Check your solution by plugging the value of the variable into the original equation.

Examples:

Example 1. Solve this equation for x. $4x + 8 = 20 - 2x$

Solution: First, bring variables to one side by adding $2x$ to both sides. Then:
$4x + 8 + 2x = 20 - 2x + 2x \rightarrow 4x + 8 + 2x = 20$.
Simplify: $6x + 8 = 20$ Now, subtract 8 from both sides of the equation:
$6x + 8 - 8 = 20 - 8 \rightarrow 6x = 12 \rightarrow$ Divide both sides by 6:
$6x = 12 \rightarrow \dfrac{6x}{6} = \dfrac{12}{6} \rightarrow x = 2$

Let's check this solution by substituting the value of 2 for x in the original equation:
$x = 2 \rightarrow 4x + 8 = 20 - 2x \rightarrow 4(2) + 8 = 20 - 2(2) \rightarrow 16 = 16$
The answer $x = 2$ is correct.

Example 2. Solve this equation for x. $-5x + 4 = 24$

Solution: Subtract 4 from both sides of the equation.
$-5x + 4 = 24 \rightarrow -5x + 4 - 4 = 24 - 4 \rightarrow -5x = 20$
Divide both sides by -5, then: $-5x = 20 \rightarrow \dfrac{-5x}{-5} = \dfrac{20}{-5} \rightarrow x = -4$

Now, check the solution:
$x = -4 \rightarrow -5x + 4 = 24 \rightarrow -5(-4) + 4 = 24 \rightarrow 24 = 24$
The answer $x = -4$ is correct.

bit.ly/3nQbSEB
Find more at

System of Equations

- A system of equations contains two equations and two variables. For example, consider the system of equations: $x - y = 1, x + y = 5$

- The easiest way to solve a system of equations is using the elimination method. The elimination method uses the addition property of equality. You can add the same value to each side of an equation.

- For the first equation above, you can add $x + y$ to the left side and 5 to the right side of the first equation: $x - y + (x + y) = 1 + 5$. Now, if you simplify, you get: $x - y + (x + y) = 1 + 5 \rightarrow 2x = 6 \rightarrow x = 3$. Now, substitute 3 for the x in the first equation: $3 - y = 1$. By solving this equation, $y = 2$

Example:

What is the value of $x + y$ in this system of equations?

$$\begin{cases} 2x + 4y = 12 \\ 4x - 2y = -16 \end{cases}$$

Solution: Solving a System of Equations by Elimination:
Multiply the first equation by (-2), then add it to the second equation.

$$\begin{array}{l} -2(2x + 4y = 12) \\ 4x - 2y = -16 \end{array} \Rightarrow \begin{array}{l} -4x - 8y = -24 \\ 4x - 2y = -16 \end{array} \Rightarrow -10y = -40 \Rightarrow y = 4$$

Plug in the value of y into one of the equations and solve for x.
$2x + 4(4) = 12 \Rightarrow 2x + 16 = 12 \Rightarrow 2x = -4 \Rightarrow x = -2$
Thus, $x + y = -2 + 4 = 2$

Graphing Single–Variable Inequalities

- An inequality compares two expressions using an inequality sign.

- Inequality signs are: "less than" <, "greater than" >, "less than or equal to" ≤, and "greater than or equal to" ≥.

- To graph a single–variable inequality, find the value of the inequality on the number line.

- For less than (<) or greater than (>) draw an open circle on the value of the variable. If there is an equal sign too, then use a filled circle.

- Draw an arrow to the right for greater or to the left for less than.

Examples:

Example 1. Draw a graph for this inequality. $x > 2$

Solution: Since the variable is greater than 2, then we need to find 2 on the number line and draw an open circle on it. Then, draw an arrow to the right.

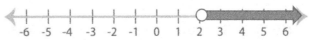

Example 2. Graph this inequality. $x \leq -3$.

Solution: Since the variable is less than or equal to −3, then we need to find −3 in the number line and draw a filled circle on it. Then, draw an arrow to the left.

One–Step Inequalities

- An inequality compares two expressions using an inequality sign.

- Inequality signs are: "less than" <, "greater than" >, "less than or equal to" ≤, and "greater than or equal to" ≥.

- You only need to perform one Math operation to solve the one-step inequalities.

- To solve one-step inequalities, find the inverse (opposite) operation is being performed.

- For dividing or multiplying both sides by negative numbers, flip the direction of the inequality sign.

Examples:

Example 1. Solve this inequality for x. $x + 5 \geq 4$

Solution: The inverse (opposite) operation of addition is subtraction. In this inequality, 5 is added to x. To isolate x we need to subtract 5 from both sides of the inequality.
Then: $x + 5 \geq 4 \rightarrow x + 5 - 5 \geq 4 - 5 \rightarrow x \geq -1$. The solution is: $x \geq -1$

Example 2. Solve the inequality. $x - 3 > -6$.

Solution: 3 is subtracted from x. Add 3 to both sides.
$x - 3 > -6 \rightarrow x - 3 + 3 > -6 + 3 \rightarrow x > -3$

Example 3. Solve. $4x \leq -8$.

Solution: 4 is multiplied to x. Divide both sides by 4.
Then: $4x \leq -8 \rightarrow \frac{4x}{4} \leq \frac{-8}{4} \rightarrow x \leq -2$

Example 4. Solve. $-3x \leq 6$.

Solution: -3 is multiplied to x. Divide both sides by -3. Remember when dividing or multiplying both sides of an inequality by negative numbers, flip the direction of the inequality sign.
Then: $-3x \leq 6 \rightarrow \frac{-3x}{-3} \geq \frac{6}{-3} \rightarrow x \geq -2$

bit.ly/3rrElgL
Find more at

Multi−Step Inequalities

- To solve a multi-step inequality, combine "like" terms on one side.

- Bring variables to one side by adding or subtracting.

- Isolate the variable.

- Simplify using the inverse of addition or subtraction.

- Simplify further by using the inverse of multiplication or division.

- For dividing or multiplying both sides by negative numbers, flip the direction of the inequality sign.

Examples:

Example 1. Solve this inequality. $8x - 2 \leq 14$

Solution: In this inequality, 2 is subtracted from $8x$. The inverse of subtraction is addition. Add 2 to both sides of the inequality:

$8x - 2 + 2 \leq 14 + 2 \rightarrow 8x \leq 16$

Now, divide both sides by 8. Then: $8x \leq 16 \rightarrow \frac{8x}{8} \leq \frac{16}{8} \rightarrow x \leq 2$

The solution of this inequality is $x \leq 2$.

Example 2. Solve this inequality. $3x + 9 < 12$

Solution: First, subtract 9 from both sides: $3x + 9 - 9 < 12 - 9$

Then simplify: $3x + 9 - 9 < 12 - 9 \rightarrow 3x < 3$

Now divide both sides by 3: $\frac{3x}{3} < \frac{3}{3} \rightarrow x < 1$

Example 3. Solve this inequality. $-5x + 3 \geq 8$

Solution: First, subtract 3 from both sides:

$-5x + 3 - 3 \geq 8 - 3 \rightarrow -5x \geq 5$

Divide both sides by -5. Remember that you need to flip the direction of inequality sign. $-5x \geq 5 \rightarrow \frac{-5x}{-5} \leq \frac{5}{-5} \rightarrow x \leq -1$

bit.ly/2WK1xOr

Find more at

Chapter 8: Practices

✍ Solve each equation. (One−Step Equations)

1) $x + 6 = 3 \rightarrow x =$ ____

2) $5 = 11 - x \rightarrow x =$ ____

3) $-3 = 8 + x \rightarrow x =$ ____

4) $x - 2 = -7 \rightarrow x =$ ____

5) $-15 = x + 6 \rightarrow x =$ ____

6) $10 - x = -2 \rightarrow x =$ ____

7) $22 - x = -9 \rightarrow x =$ ____

8) $-4 + x = 28 \rightarrow x =$ ____

9) $11 - x = -7 \rightarrow x =$ ____

10) $35 - x = -7 \rightarrow x =$ ____

✍ Solve each equation. (Multi−Step Equations)

11) $4(x + 2) = 12 \rightarrow x =$ ____

12) $-6(6 - x) = 12 \rightarrow x =$ ____

13) $5 = -5 (x + 2) \rightarrow x =$ ____

14) $-10 = 2(4 + x) \rightarrow x =$ ____

15) $4(x + 2) = -12, x =$ ____

16) $-6(3 + 2x) = 30, x =$ ____

17) $-3(4 - x) = 12, x =$ ____

18) $-4(6 - x) = 16, x =$ ____

✍ Solve each system of equations.

19) $\begin{cases} x + 6y = 32 \\ x + 3y = 17 \end{cases}$ $x =$ ____ $y =$ ____

20) $\begin{cases} 3x + y = 15 \\ x + 2y = 10 \end{cases}$ $x =$ ____ $y =$ ____

21) $\begin{cases} 3x + 5y = 17 \\ 2x + y = 9 \end{cases}$ $x =$ ____ $y =$ ____

22) $\begin{cases} 5x - 2y = -8 \\ -6x + 2y = 10 \end{cases}$ $x =$ ____ $y =$ ____

✍ **Draw a graph for each inequality.**

23) $x \leq -3$

24) $x > -5$

✍ **Solve each inequality and graph it.**

25) $x - 2 \geq -2$ ⟵─┼─┼─┼─┼─┼─┼─┼─┼─┼─┼─┼─┼─⟶
                      -6 -5 -4 -3 -2 -1   0   1   2   3   4   5   6

26) $2x - 3 < 9$ ⟵─┼─┼─┼─┼─┼─┼─┼─┼─┼─┼─┼─┼─⟶
                      -6 -5 -4 -3 -2 -1   0   1   2   3   4   5   6

✍ **Solve each inequality.**

27) $x + 13 > 4$ 35) $10 + 5x < -15$

28) $x + 6 > 5$ 36) $6(6 + x) \geq -18$

29) $-12 + 2x \leq 26$ 37) $2(x - 5) \geq -14$

30) $-2 + 8x \leq 14$ 38) $6(x + 4) < -12$

31) $6 + 4x \leq 18$ 39) $3(x - 8) \geq -48$

32) $4(x + 3) \geq -12$ 40) $-(6 - 4x) > -30$

33) $2(6 + x) \geq -12$ 41) $2(2 + 2x) > -60$

34) $3(x - 5) < -6$ 42) $-3(4 + 2x) > -24$

Effortless
Math
Education

Chapter 8: Answers

1)	-3	9)	18	17)	8
2)	6	10)	42	18)	10
3)	-11	11)	1	19)	$x = 2, y = 5$
4)	-5	12)	8	20)	$x = 4, y = 3$
5)	-21	13)	-3	21)	$x = 4, y = 1$
6)	12	14)	-9	22)	$x = -2, y = -1$
7)	31	15)	-5		
8)	32	16)	-4		

23) $x \leq -3$

24) $x > -5$

25) $x \geq 0$

26) $x < 6$

27)	$x > -9$	31)	$x \leq 3$	37)	$x \geq -2$
28)	$x > -1$	32)	$x \geq -6$	38)	$x < -6$
29)	$x \leq 19$	33)	$x \geq -12$	39)	$x \geq -8$
30)	$x \leq 2$	34)	$x < 3$	40)	$x > -6$
		35)	$x < -5$	41)	$x > -16$
		36)	$x \geq -9$	42)	$x < 2$

CHAPTER

9 Lines and Slope

Math topics that you'll learn in this chapter:

- ☑ Finding Slope
- ☑ Graphing Lines Using Slope–Intercept Form
- ☑ Writing Linear Equations
- ☑ Finding Midpoint
- ☑ Finding Distance of Two Points
- ☑ Graphing Linear Inequalities

77

Finding Slope

- The slope of a line represents the direction of a line on the coordinate plane.

- A coordinate plane contains two perpendicular number lines. The horizontal line is x and the vertical line is y. The point at which the two axes intersect is called the origin. An ordered pair (x, y) shows the location of a point.

- A line on a coordinate plane can be drawn by connecting two points.

- To find the slope of a line, we need the equation of the line or two points on the line.

- The slope of a line with two points A (x_1, y_1) and B (x_2, y_2) can be found by using this formula: $\frac{y_2 - y_1}{x_2 - x_1} = \frac{rise}{run}$

- The equation of a line is typically written as $y = mx + b$ where m is the slope and b is the y-intercept.

Examples:

Example 1. Find the slope of the line through these two points:

A$(1, -6)$ and $B(3, 2)$.

Solution: Slope $= \frac{y_2 - y_1}{x_2 - x_1}$. Let (x_1, y_1) be A$(1, -6)$ and (x_2, y_2) be $B(3, 2)$.

(Remember, you can choose any point for (x_1, y_1) and (x_2, y_2)).
Then: slope $= \frac{y_2 - y_1}{x_2 - x_1} = \frac{2 - (-6)}{3 - 1} = \frac{8}{2} = 4$

The slope of the line through these two points is 4.

Example 2. Find the slope of the line with equation $y = -2x + 8$

Solution: when the equation of a line is written in the form of $y = mx + b$, the slope is m. In this line: $y = -2x + 8$, the slope is -2.

Graphing Lines Using Slope–Intercept Form

-   Slope–intercept form of a line: given the slope m and the y–intercept (the intersection of the line and y-axis) b, then the equation of the line is:

$$y = mx + b$$

-   To draw the graph of a linear equation in a slope-intercept form on the xy coordinate plane, find two points on the line by plugging two values for x and calculating the values of y.

-   You can also use the slope (m) and one point to graph the line.

Example:

Sketch the graph of $y = 2x - 4$.

Solution: To graph this line, we need to find two points. When x is zero the value of y is -4. And when x is 2 the value of y is 0.

$$x = 0 \rightarrow y = 2(0) - 4 = -4,$$
$$y = 0 \rightarrow 0 = 2x - 4 \rightarrow x = 2$$

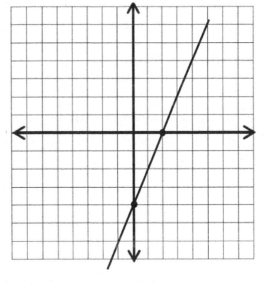

Now, we have two points:
$(0, -4)$ and $(2, 0)$.
Find the points on the coordinate plane and graph the line. Remember that the slope of the line is 2.

Writing Linear Equations

- The equation of a line in slope-intercept form: $y = mx + b$

- To write the equation of a line, first identify the slope.

- Find the y-intercept. This can be done by substituting the slope and the coordinates of a point (x, y) on the line.

Examples:

Example 1. What is the equation of the line that passes through $(3, -4)$ and has a slope of 6?

Solution: The general slope-intercept form of the equation of a line is $y = mx + b$, where m is the slope and b is the y-intercept.
By substitution of the given point and given slope:
$y = mx + b \rightarrow -4 = (3)(6) + b$. So, $b = -4 - 18 = -22$, and the required equation is $y = 6x - 22$

Example 2. Write the equation of the line through two points $A(3,1)$ and $B(-2,6)$.

Solution: First, find the slope: $Slop = \frac{y_2 - y_1}{x_2 - x_1} = \frac{6-1}{-2-3} = \frac{5}{-5} = -1 \rightarrow m = -1$
To find the value of b, use either points and plug in the values of x and y in the equation. The answer will be the same: $y = -x + b$. Let's check both points. Then: $(3,1) \rightarrow y = mx + b \rightarrow 1 = -1(3) + b \rightarrow b = 4$
$(-2,6) \rightarrow y = mx + b \rightarrow 6 = -1(-2) + b \rightarrow b = 4$.
The y-intercept of the line is 4. The equation of the line is: $y = -x + 4$

Example 3. What is the equation of the line that passes through $(4, -1)$ and has a slope of 4?

Solution: The general slope-intercept form of the equation of a line is $y = mx + b$, where m is the slope and b is the y-intercept. By substitution of the given point and given slope:$y = mx + b \rightarrow -1 = (4)(4) + b$
So, $b = -1 - 16 = -17$, and the equation of the line is: $y = 4x - 17$.

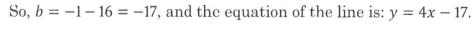

Finding Midpoint

- The middle of a line segment is its midpoint.

- The Midpoint of two endpoints A (x_1, y_1) and B (x_2, y_2) can be found using this formula: M $\left(\frac{x_1+x_2}{2}, \frac{y_1+y_2}{2}\right)$

Examples:

Example 1. Find the midpoint of the line segment with the given endpoints. $(2, -4), (6, 8)$

Solution: Midpoint $= \left(\frac{x_1+x_2}{2}, \frac{y_1+y_2}{2}\right) \rightarrow (x_1, y_1) = (2, -4)$ and $(x_2, y_2) = (6, 8)$

Midpoint $= \left(\frac{2+6}{2}, \frac{-4+8}{2}\right) \rightarrow \left(\frac{8}{2}, \frac{4}{2}\right) \rightarrow M(4, 2)$

Example 2. Find the midpoint of the line segment with the given endpoints. $(-2, 3), (6, -7)$

Solution: Midpoint $= \left(\frac{x_1+x_2}{2}, \frac{y_1+y_2}{2}\right) \rightarrow (x_1, y_1) = (-2, 3)$ and $(x_2, y_2) = (6, -7)$

Midpoint $= \left(\frac{-2+6}{2}, \frac{3-7}{2}\right) \rightarrow \left(\frac{4}{2}, \frac{-4}{2}\right) \rightarrow M(2, -2)$

Example 3. Find the midpoint of the line segment with the given endpoints. $(7, -4), (1, 8)$

Solution: Midpoint $= \left(\frac{x_1+x_2}{2}, \frac{y_1+y_2}{2}\right) \rightarrow (x_1, y_1) = (7, -4)$ and $(x_2, y_2) = (1, 8)$

Midpoint $= \left(\frac{7+1}{2}, \frac{-4+8}{2}\right) \rightarrow \left(\frac{8}{2}, \frac{4}{2}\right) \rightarrow M(4, 2)$

Example 4. Find the midpoint of the line segment with the given endpoints. $(6, 3), (10, -9)$

Solution: Midpoint $= \left(\frac{x_1+x_2}{2}, \frac{y_1+y_2}{2}\right) \rightarrow (x_1, y_1) = (6, 3)$ and $(x_2, y_2) = (10, -9)$

Midpoint $= \left(\frac{6+10}{2}, \frac{3-9}{2}\right) \rightarrow \left(\frac{16}{2}, \frac{-6}{2}\right) \rightarrow M(8, -3)$

bit.ly/3nPdnTq

Find more at

Finding Distance of Two Points

- Use the following formula to find the distance of two points with the coordinates A (x_1, y_1) and B (x_2, y_2):

$$d = \sqrt{(x_2 - x_1)^2 + (y_2 - y_1)^2}$$

Examples:

Example 1. Find the distance between $(4, 2)$ and $(-5, -10)$.

Solution: Use distance of two points formula: $d = \sqrt{(x_2 - x_1)^2 + (y_2 - y_1)^2}$

$(x_1, y_1) = (4, 2)$ and $(x_2, y_2) = (-5, -10)$. Then: $d = \sqrt{(x_2 - x_1)^2 + (y_2 - y_1)^2} \rightarrow$

$$d = \sqrt{(-5 - 4)^2 + (-10 - 2)^2} = \sqrt{(-9)^2 + (-12)^2} = \sqrt{81 + 144} = \sqrt{225} = 15$$

Then: $d = 15$

Example 2. Find the distance of two points $(-1, 5)$ and $(-3, -6)$.

Solution: Use distance of two points formula: $d = \sqrt{(x_2 - x_1)^2 + (y_2 - y_1)^2}$

$(x_1, y_1) = (-1, 5)$, and $(x_2, y_2) = (-3, -6)$

Then: $= \sqrt{(x_2 - x_1)^2 + (y_2 - y_1)^2} \rightarrow d = \sqrt{(-3 - (-1))^2 + (-6 - (5))^2} =$

$\sqrt{(-2)^2 + (-11)^2} = \sqrt{4 + 121} = \sqrt{125} = 5\sqrt{5}$. Then: $d = 5\sqrt{5}$

Example 3. Find the distance between $(-6, 5)$ and $(-2, 2)$.

Solution: Use distance of two points formula: $d = \sqrt{(x_2 - x_1)^2 + (y_2 - y_1)^2}$

$(x_1, y_1) = (-6, 5)$ and $(x_2, y_2) = (-2, 2)$. Then: $d = \sqrt{(x_2 - x_1)^2 + (y_2 - y_1)^2}$

$$d = \sqrt{(-2 - (-6))^2 + (2 - 5)^2} = \sqrt{(4)^2 + (-3)^2} = \sqrt{16 + 9} = \sqrt{25} = 5$$

Graphing Linear Inequalities

- To graph a linear inequality, first draw a graph of the "equals" line.

- Use a dash line for less than (<) and greater than (>) signs and a solid line for less than and equal to (≤) and greater than and equal to (≥).

- Choose a testing point. (it can be any point on both sides of the line.)

- Put the value of (x, y) of that point in the inequality. If that works, that part of the line is the solution. If the values don't work, then the other part of the line is the solution.

Example:

Sketch the graph of inequality: $y < 2x + 4$

Solution: To draw the graph of $y < 2x + 4$, you first need to graph the line:

$y = 2x + 4$

Since there is a less than (<) sign, draw a dash line.

The slope is 2 and y-intercept is 4.

Then, choose a testing point and substitute the value of x and y from that point into the inequality. The easiest point to test is the origin: $(0, 0)$

$(0, 0) \rightarrow y < 2x + 4 \rightarrow 0 < 2(0) + 4 \rightarrow 0 < 4$

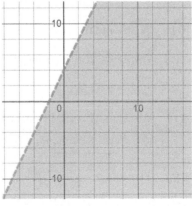

This is correct! 0 is less than 4. So, this part of the line (on the right side) is the solution of this inequality.

Find more at bit.ly/2S4lMr9

Chapter 9: Practices

✎ Find the slope of each line.

1) $y = x - 5$

2) $y = 2x + 6$

3) $y = -5x - 8$

4) Line through $(2, 6)$ *and* $(5, 0)$

5) Line through $(8, 0)$ *and* $(-4, 3)$

6) Line through $(-2, -4)$ *and* $(-4, 8)$

✎ Sketch the graph of each line. (Using Slope−Intercept Form)

7) $y = x + 4$

8) $y = 2x - 5$

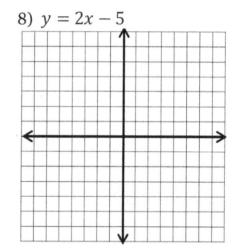

✎ Solve.

9) What is the equation of a line with slope 4 and intercept 16? _____

10) What is the equation of a line with slope 3 and passes through point $(1, 5)$?

_____

11) What is the equation of a line with slope −5 and passes through point $(-2, 7)$?

_____

12) The slope of a line is −4 and it passes through point $(-6, 2)$. What is the equation of the line? _____

13) The slope of a line is −3 and it passes through point $(-3, -6)$. What is the equation of the line? _____

**Effortless
Math
Education**

✎ **Sketch the graph of each linear inequality.**

14) $y > 2x - 2$

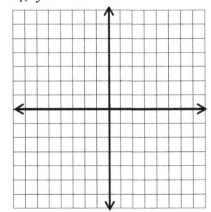

15) $y < -x + 3$

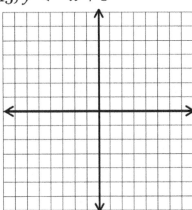

✎ **Find the midpoint of the line segment with the given endpoints.**

16) $(5, 0), (1, 4)$

17) $(2, 3), (4, 7)$

18) $(8, 1), (2, 5)$

19) $(5, 10), (3, 6)$

20) $(4, -1), (-2, 7)$

21) $(2, -5), (4, 1)$

22) $(7, 6), (-5, 2)$

23) $(-2, 8), (4, -6)$

✎ **Find the distance between each pair of points.**

24) $(-2, 8), (-6, 8)$

25) $(4, -4), (14, 20)$

26) $(-1, 9), (-5, 6)$

27) $(0, 3), (4, 3)$

28) $(0, -2), (5, 10)$

29) $(4, 3), (7, -1)$

30) $(2, 6), (10, -9)$

31) $(3, 3), (6, -1)$

32) $(-2, -12), (14, 18)$

33) $(2, -2), (12, 22)$

**Effortless
Math
Education**

Chapter 9: Answers

1) 1

2) 2

3) −5

4) −2

5) $-\frac{1}{4}$

6) −6

7) $y = x + 4$

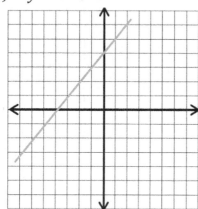

8) $y = 2x - 5$

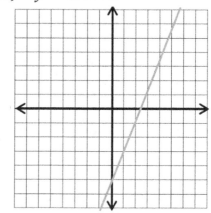

9) $y = 4x + 16$

10) $y = 3x + 2$

11) $y = -5x - 3$

12) $y = -4x - 22$

13) $y = -3x - 15$

14) $y > 2x - 2$

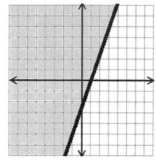

15) $y < -x + 3$

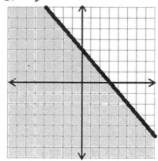

16) $(3, 2)$

17) $(3, 5)$

18) $(5, 3)$

19) $(4, 8)$

20) $(1, 3)$

21) $(3, -2)$

22) $(1, 4)$

23) $(1, 1)$

24) 4

25) 26

26) 5

27) 4

28) 13

29) 5

30) 17

31) 5

32) 34

33) 26

CHAPTER

10 Polynomials

Math topics that you'll learn in this chapter:

- ☑ Simplifying Polynomials
- ☑ Adding and Subtracting Polynomials
- ☑ Multiplying Monomials
- ☑ Multiplying and Dividing Monomials
- ☑ Multiplying a Polynomial and a Monomial
- ☑ Multiplying Binomials
- ☑ Factoring Trinomials

Simplifying Polynomials

- To simplify Polynomials, find "like" terms. (they have same variables with same power).

- Use "FOIL". (First–Out–In–Last) for binomials:

$$(x + a)(x + b) = x^2 + (b + a)x + ab$$

- Add or Subtract "like" terms using order of operation.

Examples:

Example 1. Simplify this expression. $x(4x + 7) - 2x =$

Solution: Use Distributive Property: $x(4x + 7) = 4x^2 + 7x$

Now, combine like terms: $x(4x + 7) - 2x = 4x^2 + 7x - 2x = 4x^2 + 5x$

Example 2. Simplify this expression. $(x + 3)(x + 5) =$

Solution: First, apply the FOIL method: $(a + b)(c + d) = ac + ad + bc + bd$

$(x + 3)(x + 5) = x^2 + 5x + 3x + 15$

Now combine like terms: $x^2 + 5x + 3x + 15 = x^2 + 8x + 15$

Example 3. Simplify this expression. $2x(x - 5) - 3x^2 + 6x =$

Solution: Use Distributive Property: $2x(x - 5) = 2x^2 - 10x$

Then: $2x(x - 5) - 3x^2 + 6x = 2x^2 - 10x - 3x^2 + 6x$

Now combine like terms: $2x^2 - 3x^2 = -x^2$, and $-10x + 6x = -4x$

The simplified form of the expression: $2x^2 - 10x - 3x^2 + 6 = -x^2 - 4x$

Adding and Subtracting Polynomials

- Adding polynomials is just a matter of combining like terms, with some order of operations considerations thrown in.

- Be careful with the minus signs, and don't confuse addition and multiplication!

- For subtracting polynomials, sometimes you need to use the Distributive Property: $a(b + c) = ab + ac$, $a(b - c) = ab - ac$

Examples:

Example 1. Simplify the expressions. $(x^2 - 2x^3) - (x^3 - 3x^2) =$

Solution: First, use Distributive Property:
$$-(x^3 - 3x^2) = -x^3 + 3x^2$$
$\rightarrow (x^2 - 2x^3) - (x^3 - 3x^2) = x^2 - 2x^3 - x^3 + 3x^2$
Now combine like terms: $-2x^3 - x^3 = -3x^3$ and $x^2 + 3x^2 = 4x^2$
Then: $(x^2 - 2x^3) - (x^3 - 3x^2) = x^2 - 2x^3 - x^3 + 3x^2 = -3x^3 + 4x^2$

Example 2. Add expressions. $(3x^3 - 5) + (4x^3 - 2x^2) =$

Solution: Remove parentheses:
$(3x^3 - 5) + (4x^3 - 2x^2) = 3x^3 - 5 + 4x^3 - 2x^2$
Now combine like terms: $3x^3 - 5 + 4x^3 - 2x^2 = 7x^3 - 2x^2 - 5$

Example 3. Simplify the expressions. $(-4x^2 - 2x^3) - (5x^2 + 2x^3) =$

Solution: First, use Distributive Property:
$-(5x^2 + 2x^3) = -5x^2 - 2x^3 \rightarrow (-4x^2 - 2x^3) - (5x^2 + 2x^3)$
$$= -4x^2 - 2x^3 - 5x^2 - 2x^3$$
Now combine like terms and write in standard form:
$-4x^2 - 2x^3 - 5x^2 - 2x^3 = -4x^3 - 9x^2$

bit.ly/2KUqHqQ

Find more at

Multiplying Monomials

- A monomial is a polynomial with just one term: Examples: $2x$ or $7y^2$.

- When you multiply monomials, first multiply the coefficients (a number placed before and multiplying the variable) and then multiply the variables using multiplication property of exponents.

$$x^a \times x^b = x^{a+b}$$

Examples:

Example 1. Multiply expressions. $2xy^3 \times 6x^4y^2$

Solution: Find the same variables and use multiplication property of exponents: $x^a \times x^b = x^{a+b}$
$x \times x^4 = x^{1+4} = x^5$ and $y^3 \times y^2 = y^{3+2} = y^5$
Then, multiply coefficients and variables: $2xy^3 \times 6x^4y^2 = 12x^5y^5$

Example 2. Multiply expressions. $7a^3b^8 \times 3a^6b^4 =$

Solution: Use the multiplication property of exponents: $x^a \times x^b = x^{a+b}$
$a^3 \times a^6 = a^{3+6} = a^9$ and $b^8 \times b^4 = b^{8+4} = b^{12}$
Then: $7a^3b^8 \times 3a^6b^4 = 21a^9b^{12}$

Example 3. Multiply. $5x^2y^4z^3 \times 4x^4y^7z^5$

Solution: Use the multiplication property of exponents: $x^a \times x^b = x^{a+b}$
$x^2 \times x^4 = x^{2+4} = x^6$, $y^4 \times y^7 = y^{4+7} = y^{11}$ and $z^3 \times z^5 = z^{3+5} = z^8$
Then: $5x^2y^4z^3 \times 4x^4y^7z^5 = 20x^6y^{11}z^8$

Example 4. Simplify. $(-6a^7b^4)(4a^8b^5) =$

Solution: Use the multiplication property of exponents: $x^a \times x^b = x^{a+b}$
$a^7 \times a^8 = a^{7+8} = a^{15}$ and $b^4 \times b^5 = b^{4+5} = b^9$
    Then: $(-6a^7b^4)(4a^8b^5) = -24a^{15}b^9$

Multiplying and Dividing Monomials

- When you divide or multiply two monomials, you need to divide or multiply their coefficients and then divide or multiply their variables.

- In case of exponents with the same base, for Division, subtract their powers, for Multiplication, add their powers.

- Exponent's Multiplication and Division rules:

$$x^a \times x^b = x^{a+b}, \qquad \frac{x^a}{x^b} = x^{a-b}$$

Examples:

Example 1. Multiply expressions. $(3x^5)(9x^4) =$

Solution: Use multiplication property of exponents:
$x^a \times x^b = x^{a+b} \rightarrow x^5 \times x^4 = x^9$
Then: $(3x^5)(9x^4) = 27x^9$

Example 2. Divide expressions. $\frac{12x^4y^6}{6xy^2} =$

Solution: Use division property of exponents:
$\frac{x^a}{x^b} = x^{a-b} \rightarrow \frac{x^4}{x} = x^{4-1} = x^3$ and $\frac{y^6}{y^2} = y^{6-2} = y^4$
Then: $\frac{12x^4y^6}{6xy^2} = 2x^3y^4$

Example 3. Divide expressions. $\frac{49a^6b^9}{7a^3b^4} =$

Solution: Use division property of exponents:
$\frac{x^a}{x^b} = x^{a-b} \rightarrow \frac{a^6}{a^3} = a^{6-3} = a^3$ and $\frac{b^9}{b^4} = b^{9-4} = b^5$
Then: $\frac{49a^6b^9}{7a^3b^4} = 7a^3b^5$

Multiplying a Polynomial and a Monomial

- When multiplying monomials, use the product rule for exponents.

$$x^a \times x^b = x^{a+b}$$

- When multiplying a monomial by a polynomial, use the distributive property.

$$a \times (b + c) = a \times b + a \times c = ab + ac$$
$$a \times (b - c) = a \times b - a \times c = ab - ac$$

Examples:

Example 1. Multiply expressions. $6x(2x + 5)$

Solution: Use Distributive Property:

$6x(2x + 5) = 6x \times 2x + 6x \times 5 = 12x^2 + 30x$

Example 2. Multiply expressions. $x(3x^2 + 4y^2)$

Solution: Use Distributive Property:

$x(3x^2 + 4y^2) = x \times 3x^2 + x \times 4y^2 = 3x^3 + 4xy^2$

Example 3. Multiply. $-x(-2x^2 + 4x + 5)$

Solution: Use Distributive Property:

$-x(-2x^2 + 4x + 5) = (-x)(-2x^2) + (-x) \times (4x) + (-x) \times (5) =$

Now simplify:

$(-x)(-2x^2) + (-x) \times (4x) + (-x) \times (5) = 2x^3 - 4x^2 - 5x$

Multiplying Binomials

- A binomial is a polynomial that is the sum or the difference of two terms, each of which is a monomial.

- To multiply two binomials, use the "FOIL" method. (First–Out–In–Last)

$$(x + a)(x + b) = x \times x + x \times b + a \times x + a \times b = x^2 + bx + ax + ab$$

Examples:

Example 1. Multiply Binomials. $(x + 3)(x - 2) =$

Solution: Use "FOIL". (First–Out–In–Last):
$(x + 3)(x - 2) = x^2 - 2x + 3x - 6$
Then combine like terms: $x^2 - 2x + 3x - 6 = x^2 + x - 6$

Example 2. Multiply. $(x + 6)(x + 4) =$

Solution: Use "FOIL". (First–Out–In–Last):
$(x + 6)(x + 4) = x^2 + 4x + 6x + 24$
Then simplify: $x^2 + 4x + 6x + 24 = x^2 + 10x + 24$

Example 3. Multiply. $(x + 5)(x - 7) =$

Solution: Use "FOIL". (First–Out–In–Last):
$(x + 5)(x - 7) = x^2 - 7x + 5x - 35$
Then simplify: $x^2 - 7x + 5x - 35 = x^2 - 2x - 35$

Example 4. Multiply Binomials. $(x - 9)(x - 5) =$

Solution: Use "FOIL". (First–Out–In–Last):
$(x - 9)(x - 5) = x^2 - 5x - 9x + 45$
Then combine like terms: $x^2 - 5x - 9x + 45 = x^2 - 14x + 45$

bit.ly/3aCsOFL
Find more at

Factoring Trinomials

To factor trinomials, you can use following methods:

- "FOIL": $(x + a)(x + b) = x^2 + (b + a)x + ab$

- "Difference of Squares":

$$a^2 - b^2 = (a + b)(a - b)$$
$$a^2 + 2ab + b^2 = (a + b)(a + b)$$
$$a^2 - 2ab + b^2 = (a - b)(a - b)$$

- "Reverse FOIL": $x^2 + (b + a)x + ab = (x + a)(x + b)$

Examples:

Example 1. Factor this trinomial. $x^2 - 2x - 8$

Solution: Break the expression into groups. You need to find two numbers that their product is -8 and their sum is -2. (remember "Reverse FOIL": $x^2 + (b + a)x + ab = (x + a)(x + b)$). Those two numbers are 2 and -4. Then: $x^2 - 2x - 8 = (x^2 + 2x) + (-4x - 8)$
Now factor out x from $x^2 + 2x : x(x + 2)$, and factor out -4 from $-4x - 8: -4(x + 2)$; Then: $(x^2 + 2x) + (-4x - 8) = x(x + 2) - 4(x + 2)$
Now factor out like term: $(x + 2)$. Then: $(x + 2)(x - 4)$

Example 2. Factor this trinomial. $x^2 - 2x - 24$

Solution: Break the expression into groups: $(x^2 + 4x) + (-6x - 24)$
Now factor out x from $x^2 + 4x : x(x + 4)$, and factor out -6 from $-6x - 24: -6(x + 4)$; Then: $(x + 4) - 6(x + 4)$, now factor out like term: $(x + 4) \rightarrow x(x + 4) - 6(x + 4) = (x + 4)(x - 6)$

Find more at bit.ly/38EpdJA

Chapter 10: Practices

✑ Simplify each polynomial.

1) $3(6x + 4) =$

2) $5(3x - 8) =$

3) $x(7x + 2) + 9x =$

4) $6x(x + 3) + 5x =$

5) $6x(3x + 1) - 5x =$

6) $x(3x - 4) + 3x^2 - 6 =$

7) $x^2 - 5 - 3x(x + 8) =$

8) $2x^2 + 7 - 6x(2x + 5) =$

✑ Add or subtract polynomials.

9) $(x^2 + 3) + (2x^2 - 4) =$

10) $(3x^2 - 6x) - (x^2 + 8x) =$

11) $(4x^3 - 3x^2) + (2x^3 - 5x^2) =$

12) $(6x^3 - 7x) - (5x^3 - 3x) =$

13) $(10x^3 + 4x^2) + (14x^2 - 8) =$

14) $(4x^3 - 9) - (3x^3 - 7x^2) =$

15) $(9x^3 + 3x) - (6x^3 - 4x) =$

16) $(7x^3 - 5x) - (3x^3 + 5x) =$

✑ Find the products. (Multiplying Monomials)

17) $3x^2 \times 8x^3 =$

18) $2x^4 \times 9x^3 =$

19) $-4a^4b \times 2ab^3 =$

20) $(-7x^3yz) \times (3xy^2z^4) =$

21) $-2a^5bc \times 6a^2b^4 =$

22) $9u^3t^2 \times (-2ut) =$

23) $12x^2z \times 3xy^3 =$

24) $11x^3z \times 5xy^5 =$

25) $-6a^3bc \times 5a^4b^3 =$

26) $-4x^6y^2 \times (-12xy) =$

Effortless
Math
Education

✎ **Simplify each expression. (Multiplying and Dividing Monomials)**

27) $(7x^2y^3)(3x^4y^2) =$

28) $(6x^3y^2)(4x^4y^3) =$

29) $(10x^8y^5)(3x^5y^7) =$

30) $(15a^3b^2)(2a^3b^8) =$

31) $\dfrac{42x^4y^2}{6x^3y} =$

32) $\dfrac{49x^5y^6}{7x^2y} =$

33) $\dfrac{63x^{15}y^{10}}{9x^8y^6} =$

34) $\dfrac{35x^8y^{12}}{5x^4y^8} =$

✎ **Find each product. (Multiplying a Polynomial and a Monomial)**

35) $3x(5x - y) =$

36) $2x(4x + y) =$

37) $7x(x - 3y) =$

38) $x(2x^2 + 2x - 4) =$

39) $5x(3x^2 + 8x + 2) =$

40) $7x(2x^2 - 9x - 5) =$

✎ **Find each product. (Multiplying Binomials)**

41) $(x - 3)(x + 3) =$

42) $(x - 6)(x + 6) =$

43) $(x + 10)(x + 4) =$

44) $(x - 6)(x + 7) =$

45) $(x + 2)(x - 5) =$

46) $(x - 10)(x + 3) =$

✎ **Factor each trinomial.**

47) $x^2 + 6x + 8 =$

48) $x^2 + 3x - 10 =$

49) $x^2 + 2x - 48 =$

50) $x^2 - 10x + 16 =$

51) $2x^2 - 10x + 12 =$

52) $3x^2 - 10x + 3 =$

Effortless

Math

Education

Chapter 10: Answers

1) $18x + 12$

2) $15x - 40$

3) $7x^2 + 11x$

4) $6x^2 + 23x$

5) $18x^2 + x$

6) $6x^2 - 4x - 6$

7) $-2x^2 - 24x - 5$

8) $-10x^2 - 30x + 7$

9) $3x^2 - 1$

10) $2x^2 - 14x$

11) $6x^3 - 8x^2$

12) $x^3 - 4x$

13) $10x^3 + 18x^2 - 8$

14) $x^3 + 7x^2 - 9$

15) $3x^3 + 7x$

16) $4x^3 - 10x$

17) $24x^5$

18) $18x^7$

19) $-8a^5b^4$

20) $-21x^4y^3z^5$

21) $-12a^7b^5c$

22) $-18u^4t^3$

23) $36x^3y^3z$

24) $55x^4y^5z$

25) $-30a^7b^4c$

26) $48x^7y^3$

27) $21x^6y^5$

28) $24x^7y^5$

29) $30x^{13}y^{12}$

30) $30a^6b^{10}$

31) $7xy$

32) $7x^3y^5$

33) $7x^7y^4$

34) $7x^4y^4$

35) $15x^2 - 3xy$

36) $8x^2 + 2xy$

37) $7x^2 - 21xy$

38) $2x^3 + 2x^2 - 4x$

39) $15x^3 + 40x^2 + 10x$

40) $14x^3 - 63x^2 - 35x$

41) $x^2 - 9$

42) $x^2 - 36$

43) $x^2 + 14x + 40$

44) $x^2 + x - 42$

45) $x^2 - 3x - 10$

46) $x^2 - 7x - 30$

47) $(x + 4)(x + 2)$

48) $(x + 5)(x - 2)$

49) $(x - 6)(x + 8)$

50) $(x - 8)(x - 2)$

51) $(2x - 4)(x - 3)$

52) $(3x - 1)(x - 3)$

CHAPTER

11 Geometry and Solid Figures

Math topics that you'll learn in this chapter:

- ☑ The Pythagorean Theorem
- ☑ Complementary and Supplementary angles
- ☑ Parallel lines and Transversals
- ☑ Triangles
- ☑ Special Right Triangles
- ☑ Polygons
- ☑ Circles
- ☑ Trapezoids
- ☑ Cubes
- ☑ Rectangle Prisms
- ☑ Cylinder

The Pythagorean Theorem

- You can use the Pythagorean Theorem to find a missing side in a right triangle.

- In any right triangle: $a^2 + b^2 = c^2$

Examples:

Example 1. Right triangle ABC (not shown) has two legs of lengths 3 cm (AB) and 4 cm (AC). What is the length of the hypotenuse of the triangle (side BC)?

Solution: Use Pythagorean Theorem: $a^2 + b^2 = c^2$, $a = 3$, and $b = 4$

Then: $a^2 + b^2 = c^2 \rightarrow 3^2 + 4^2 = c^2 \rightarrow 9 + 16 = c^2 \rightarrow 25 = c^2 \rightarrow c = \sqrt{25} = 5$

The length of the hypotenuse is 5 cm.

Example 2. Find the hypotenuse of this triangle.

Solution: Use Pythagorean Theorem: $a^2 + b^2 = c^2$

Then: $a^2 + b^2 = c^2 \rightarrow 8^2 + 6^2 = c^2 \rightarrow 64 + 36 = c^2$

$c^2 = 100 \rightarrow c = \sqrt{100} = 10$

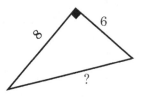

Example 3. Find the length of the missing side in this triangle.

Solution: Use Pythagorean Theorem: $a^2 + b^2 = c^2$

Then: $a^2 + b^2 = c^2 \rightarrow 12^2 + b^2 = 15^2 \rightarrow 144 + b^2 = 225 \rightarrow$

$\quad\quad\quad b^2 = 225 - 144 \rightarrow b^2 = 81 \rightarrow b = \sqrt{81} = 9$

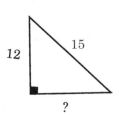

Complementary and Supplementary angles

- Two angles with a sum of 90 degrees are called complementary angles.

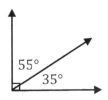

- Two angles with a sum of 180 degrees are Supplementary angles.

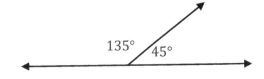

Examples:

Example 1. Find the missing angle.

Solution: Notice that the two angles form a right angle. This means that the angles are complementary, and their sum is 90.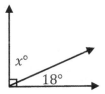

Then: $18 + x = 90 \rightarrow x = 90^{\circ} - 18^{\circ} = 72^{\circ}$

The missing angle is 72 degrees. $x = 72°$

Example 2. Angles Q and S are supplementary. What is the measure of angle Q if angle S is 35 degrees?

Solution: Q and S are supplementary $\rightarrow Q + S = 180 \rightarrow Q + 35 = 180 \rightarrow$

$$Q = 180 - 35 = 145$$

Parallel lines and Transversals

- When a line (transversal) intersects two parallel lines in the same plane, eight angles are formed. In the following diagram, a transversal intersects two parallel lines. Angles 1, 3, 5, and 7 are congruent. Angles 2, 4, 6, and 8 are also congruent.

- In the following diagram, the following angles are supplementary angles (their sum is 180):

  ❖ Angles 1 and 8

  ❖ Angles 2 and 7

  ❖ Angles 3 and 6

  ❖ Angles 4 and 5

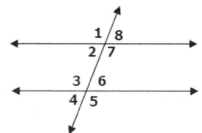

Example:

In the following diagram, two parallel lines are cut by a transversal. What is the value of x?

Solution: The two angles $3x - 15$ and $2x + 7$ are equivalent.

That is: $3x - 15 = 2x + 7$

Now, solve for x:

$3x - 15 + 15 = 2x + 7 + 15$

$\rightarrow 3x = 2x + 22 \rightarrow 3x - 2x = 2x + 22 - 2x$

$\rightarrow x = 22$

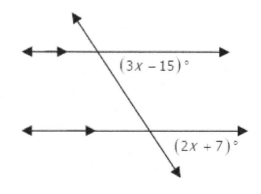

Triangles

- In any triangle, the sum of all angles is 180 degrees.

- Area of a triangle $= \frac{1}{2}\,(base \times height)$

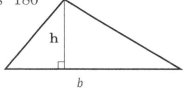

Examples:

What is the area of the following triangles?

Example 1.

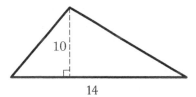

Solution: Use the area formula:

Area $= \frac{1}{2}\,(base \times height)$

$base = 14$ and $height = 10$

Area $= \frac{1}{2}\,(14 \times 10) = \frac{1}{2}\,(140) = 70$

Example 2.

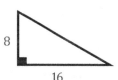

Solution: Use the area formula:

Area $= \frac{1}{2}\,(base \times height)$

$base = 16$ and $height = 8$; Area $= \frac{1}{2}\,(16 \times 8) = \frac{128}{2} = 64$

Example 3. What is the missing angle in this triangle?

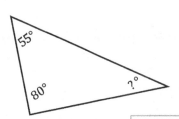

Solution:

In any triangle, the sum of all angles is 180 degrees.

Let x be the missing angle.

Then: $55 + 80 + x = 180$;

$\rightarrow 135 + x = 180 \rightarrow x = 180 - 135 = 45$

The missing angle is 45 degrees.

Special Right Triangles

- A special right triangle is a triangle whose sides are in a particular ratio. Two special right triangles are $45° - 45° - 90°$ and $30° - 60° - 90°$ triangles.

- In a special $45° - 45° - 90°$ triangle, the three angles are $45°$, $45°$ and $90°$. The lengths of the sides of this triangle are in the ratio of $1:1:\sqrt{2}$.

- In a special triangle $30° - 60° - 90°$, the three angles are $30° - 60° - 90°$. The lengths of this triangle are in the ratio of $1:\sqrt{3}:2$.

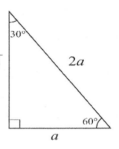

Examples:

Example 1. Find the length of the hypotenuse of a right triangle if the length of the other two sides are both 4 inches.

Solution: this is a right triangle with two equal sides. Therefore, it must be a $45° - 45° - 90°$ triangle. Two equivalent sides are 4 inches. The ratio of sides: $x:x:x\sqrt{2}$

The length of the hypotenuse is $4\sqrt{2}$ inches. $x:x:x\sqrt{2} \rightarrow 4:4:4\sqrt{2}$

Example 2. The length of the hypotenuse of a triangle is 6 inches. What are the lengths of the other two sides if one angle of the triangle is $30°$?

Solution: The hypotenuse is 6 inches and the triangle is a $30° - 60° - 90°$ triangle.

Then, one side of the triangle is 3 (it's half the side of the hypotenuse) and the other side is $3\sqrt{3}$. (it's the smallest side times $\sqrt{3}$)

$$x:x\sqrt{3}:2x \rightarrow x = 3 \rightarrow x:x\sqrt{3}:2x = 3:3\sqrt{3}:6$$

Polygons

- The perimeter of a square = $4 \times side = 4s$

- The perimeter of a rectangle= $2(width + length)$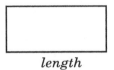

- The perimeter of trapezoid= $a + b + c + d$

- The perimeter of a regular hexagon = $6a$

- The perimeter of a parallelogram = $2(l + w)$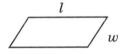

Examples:

Example 1. Find the perimeter of following regular hexagon.

Solution: Since the hexagon is regular, all sides are equal.
Then: The perimeter of The hexagon = $6 \times (one\ side)$
The perimeter of The hexagon = $6 \times (one\ side) = 6 \times 8 = 48\ m$

Example 2. Find the perimeter of following trapezoid.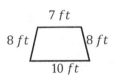

Solution: The perimeter of a trapezoid = $a + b + c + d$
The perimeter of the trapezoid = $7 + 8 + 8 + 10 = 33\ ft$

bit.ly/3nFNiGi

Find more at

Circles

- In a circle, variable *r* is usually used for the radius and *d* for diameter.

- *Area of a circle = πr² (π is about 3.14)*

- *Circumference of a circle = 2πr*

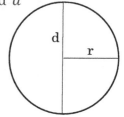

Examples:

Example 1. Find the area of this circle.

Solution:
Use area formula: *Area = πr²*
$r = 6\ in \rightarrow Area = \pi(6)^2 = 36\pi$, π = 3.14
Then: *Area* = 36 × 3.14 = 113.04 *in²*

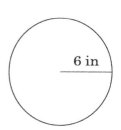

Example 2. Find the Circumference of this circle.

Solution:
Use Circumference formula: *Circumference = 2πr*
$r = 8\ cm \rightarrow Circumference = 2\pi(8) = 16\pi$
π = 3.14 Then: *Circumference* = 16 × 3.14 = 50.24 *cm*

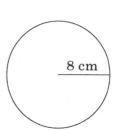

Example 3. Find the area of the circle.

Solution:
Use area formula: *Area = πr²* ,
$r = 9\ in$ then: $Area = \pi(9)^2 = 81\pi$, π = 3.14
Then: *Area* = 81 × 3.14 = 254.34 *in²*

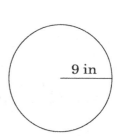

Trapezoids

- A quadrilateral with at least one pair of parallel sides is a trapezoid.

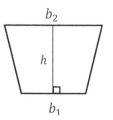

- Area of a trapezoid $= \frac{1}{2}h(b_1 + b_2)$

Examples:

Example 1. Calculate the area of this trapezoid.

Solution:

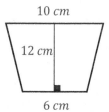

Use area formula: $A = \frac{1}{2}h(b_1 + b_2)$

$b_1 = 6 \, cm$, $b_2 = 10 \, cm$ and $h = 12 \, cm$

Then: $A = \frac{1}{2}(12)(10 + 6) = 6(16) = 96 \, cm^2$

Example 2. Calculate the area of this trapezoid.

Solution:

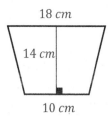

Use area formula: $A = \frac{1}{2}h(b_1 + b_2)$

$b_1 = 10 \, cm$, $b_2 = 18 \, cm$ and $h = 14 \, cm$

Then: $A = \frac{1}{2}(14)(10 + 18) = 7(28) = 196 \, cm^2$

Cubes

- A cube is a three-dimensional solid object bounded by six square sides.

- Volume is the measure of the amount of space inside of a solid figure, like a cube, ball, cylinder or pyramid.

- The volume of a cube = $(one\ side)^3$

- The surface area of a cube = $6 \times (one\ side)^2$

Examples:

Example 1. Find the volume and surface area of this cube.

Solution: Use volume formula: $volume = (one\ side)^3$
Then: $volume = (one\ side)^3 = (3)^3 = 27\ cm^3$
Use surface area formula:
$surface\ area\ of\ cube$: $6(one\ side)^2 = 6(3)^2 = 6(9) = 54\ cm^2$

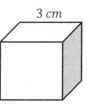
3 cm

Example 2. Find the volume and surface area of this cube.

Solution: Use volume formula: $volume = (one\ side)^3$
Then: $volume = (one\ side)^3 = (6)^3 = 216\ cm^3$
Use surface area formula:
$surface\ area\ of\ cube$: $6(one\ side)^2 = 6(6)^2 = 6(36) = 216\ cm^2$

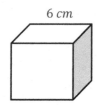
6 cm

Example 3. Find the volume and surface area of this cube.

Solution: Use volume formula: $volume = (one\ side)^3$
Then: $volume = (one\ side)^3 = (8)^3 = 512\ m^3$
Use surface area formula:
$surface\ area\ of\ cube$: $6(one\ side)^2 = 6(8)^2 = 6(64) = 384\ m^2$

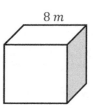
8 m

Rectangular Prisms

- A rectangular prism is a solid 3-dimensional object with six rectangular faces.

- The volume of a Rectangular prism = $Length \times Width \times Height$

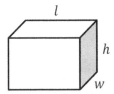

$Volume = l \times w \times h$

$Surface\ area = 2 \times (wh + lw + lh)$

Examples:

Example 1. Find the volume and surface area of this rectangular prism.

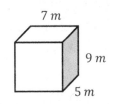

Solution: Use volume formula: $Volume = l \times w \times h$

Then: $Volume = 7 \times 5 \times 9 = 315\ m^3$

Use surface area formula: $Surface\ area = 2 \times (wh + lw + lh)$

Then: $Surface\ area = 2 \times \big((5 \times 9) + (7 \times 5) + (7 \times 9)\big)$

$$= 2 \times (45 + 35 + 63) = 2 \times (143) = 286\ m^2$$

Example 2. Find the volume and surface area of this rectangular prism.

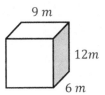

Solution: Use volume formula: $Volume = l \times w \times h$

Then: $Volume = 9 \times 6 \times 12 = 648\ m^3$

Use surface area formula: $Surface\ area = 2 \times (wh + lw + lh)$

Then: $Surface\ area = 2 \times \big((6 \times 12) + (9 \times 6) + (9 \times 12)\big)$

$$= 2 \times (72 + 54 + 108) = 2 \times (234) = 468\ m^2$$

bit.ly/3nKm2G

Find more at

Cylinder

- A cylinder is a solid geometric figure with straight parallel sides and a circular or oval cross-section.

- *Volume of a Cylinder* $= \pi(radius)^2 \times height$, $\pi \approx 3.14$

- *Surface area of a cylinder* $= 2\pi r^2 + 2\pi rh$

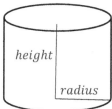

Examples:

Example 1. Find the volume and Surface area of the follow Cylinder.

Solution: Use volume formula:

$Volume = \pi(radius)^2 \times height$

Then: $Volume = \pi(4)^2 \times 10 = 16\pi \times 10 = 160\pi$

$\pi = 3.14$ then: $Volume = 160\pi = 160 \times 3.14 = 502.4 \ cm^3$

Use surface area formula: $Surface \ area = 2\pi r^2 + 2\pi rh$

Then: $2\pi(4)^2 + 2\pi(4)(10) = 2\pi(16) + 2\pi(40) = 32\pi + 80\pi = 112\pi$

$\pi = 3.14$ Then: $Surface \ area = 112 \times 3.14 = 351.68 \ cm^2$

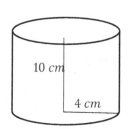

Example 2. Find the volume and Surface area of the follow Cylinder.

Solution: Use volume formula:

$Volume = \pi(radius)^2 \times height$

Then: $Volume = \pi(5)^2 \times 8 = \pi 25 \times 8 = 200\pi$

$\pi = 3.14$ then: $Volume = 200\pi = 628 \ cm^3$

Use surface area formula: $Surface \ area = 2\pi r^2 + 2\pi rh$

Then: $= 2\pi(5)^2 + 2\pi(5)(8) = 2\pi(25) + 2\pi(40) = 50\pi + 80\pi = 130\pi$

$\pi = 3.14$ then: $Surface \ area = 130 \times 3.14 = 408.2 \ cm^2$

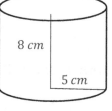

bit.ly/37LtcVM

Find more at

Chapter 11: Practices

✎ Find the missing side?

1)

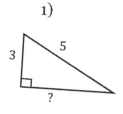

2)

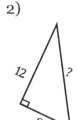

3)

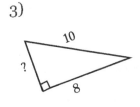

4)

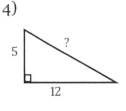

✎ Find the measure of the unknown angle in each triangle.

5)   6)   7)   8)

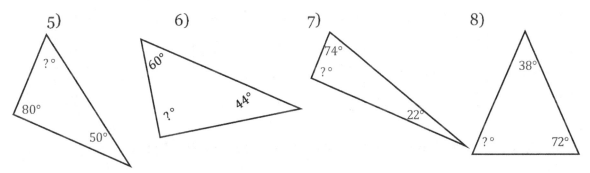

✎ Find the area of each triangle.

9)   10)   11)   12)

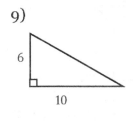

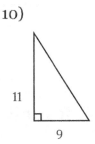

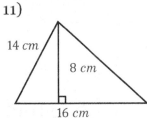

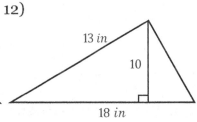

✎ Find the perimeter or circumference of each shape.

13)   14)   15)   16) *regular hexago*

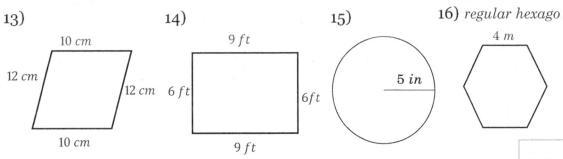

✐ **Find the area of each trapezoid.**

17)
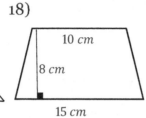
10 m
7 m
14 m

18)

10 cm
8 cm
15 cm

19)
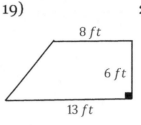
8 ft
6 ft
13 ft

20)
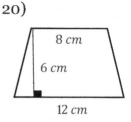
8 cm
6 cm
12 cm

✐ **Find the volume of each cube.**

21)
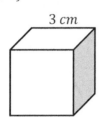
3 cm

22)
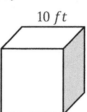
10 ft

23)
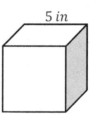
5 in

24)
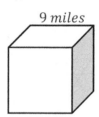
9 miles

✐ **Find the volume of each Rectangular Prism.**

25)
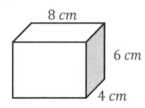
8 cm
6 cm
4 cm

26)
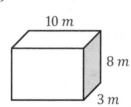
10 m
8 m
3 m

27)
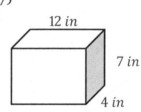
12 in
7 in
4 in

✐ **Find the volume of each Cylinder. Round your answer to the nearest tenth. (π = 3.14)**

28)
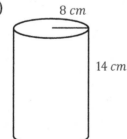
8 cm
14 cm

29)
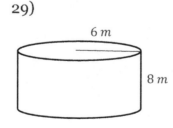
6 m
8 m

30)
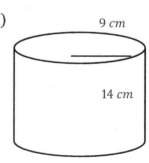
9 cm
14 cm

Effortless
Math
Education

EffortlessMath.com

**Effortless
Math
Education**

Chapter 11: Answers

1) 4

2) 15

3) 6

4) 13

5) 50

6) 76

7) 84

8) 70

9) 30

10) 49.5

11) $64\ cm^2$

12) $90\ in^2$

13) $44\ cm$

14) $30\ ft$

15) $10\ \pi \approx 31.4\ in$

16) $24\ m$

17) $84\ m^2$

18) $100\ cm^2$

19) $63\ ft^2$

20) $60\ cm^2$

21) $27\ cm^3$

22) $1{,}000\ ft^3$

23) $125\ in^3$

24) $729\ mi^3$

25) $192\ cm^3$

26) $240\ m^3$

27) $336\ in^3$

28) $2{,}813.44\ cm^3$

29) $904.32\ m^3$

30) $3{,}560.76\ cm^3$

12 Statistics

Math topics that you'll learn in this chapter:

- ☑ Mean, Median, Mode, and Range of the Given Data
- ☑ Pie Graph
- ☑ Probability Problems
- ☑ Permutations and Combinations

115

Mean, Median, Mode, and Range of the Given Data

- Mean: $\dfrac{sum\ of\ the\ data}{total\ number\ of\ data\ entires}$

- Mode: the value in the list that appears most often

- Median: is the middle number of a group of numbers arranged in order by size.

- Range: the difference of the largest value and smallest value in the list

Examples:

Example 1. What is the mode of these numbers? $5, 6, 8, 6, 8, 5, 3, 5$

Solution: Mode: the value in the list that appears most often.
Therefore, the mode is number 5. There are three number 5 in the data.

Example 2. What is the median of these numbers? $6, 11, 15, 10, 17, 20, 7$

Solution: Write the numbers in order: $6, 7, 10, 11, 15, 17, 20$
The median is the number in the middle. Therefore, the median is 11.

Example 3. What is the mean of these numbers? $7, 2, 3, 2, 4, 8, 7, 5$

Solution: Mean: $\dfrac{sum\ of\ the\ data}{total\ number\ of\ data\ entires} = \dfrac{7+2+3+2+4+8+7+5}{8} = \dfrac{38}{8} = 4.75$

Example 4. What is the range in this list? $3, 7, 12, 6, 15, 20, 8$

Solution: Range is the difference of the largest value and smallest value in the list. The largest value is 20 and the smallest value is 3.
Then: $20 - 3 = 17$

bit.ly/2KO86gg

Find more at

Pie Graph

- A Pie Chart is a circle chart divided into sectors, each sector represents the relative size of each value.

- Pie charts represent a snapshot of how a group is broken down into smaller pieces.

Examples:

A library has 750 books that include Mathematics, Physics, Chemistry, English and History. Use the following graph to answer the questions.

Example 1. What is the number of Mathematics books?

Solution: Number of total books = 750
Percent of Mathematics books = 28% = 0.28
Then, the number of Mathematics books: $0.28 \times 750 =$ 210

Example 2. What is the number of History books?

Solution: Number of total books = 750
Percent of History books = 12% = 0.12
Then: $0.12 \times 750 = 90$

Example 3. What is the number of Chemistry books?

Solution: Number of total books = 750
Percent of Chemistry books = 22% = 0.22
Then: $0.22 \times 750 = 165$

Probability Problems

- Probability is the likelihood of something happening in the future. It is expressed as a number between zero (can never happen) to 1 (will always happen).

- Probability can be expressed as a fraction, a decimal, or a percent.

- Probability formula: $Probability = \frac{number\ of\ desired\ outcomes}{number\ of\ total\ outcomes}$

Examples:

Example 1. Anita's trick–or–treat bag contains 10 pieces of chocolate, 16 suckers, 16 pieces of gum, 22 pieces of licorice. If she randomly pulls a piece of candy from her bag, what is the probability of her pulling out a piece of sucker?

Solution: Probability $= \frac{number\ of\ desired\ outcomes}{number\ of\ total\ outcomes}$

Probability of pulling out a piece of sucker $= \frac{16}{10 + 16 + 16 + 22} = \frac{16}{64} = \frac{1}{4}$

Example 2. A bag contains 20 balls: four green, five black, eight blue, a brown, a red and one white. If 19 balls are removed from the bag at random, what is the probability that a brown ball has been removed?

Solution: If 19 balls are removed from the bag at random, there will be one ball in the bag. The probability of choosing a brown ball is 1 out of 20. Therefore, the probability of not choosing a brown ball is 19 out of 20 and the probability of having not a brown ball after removing 19 balls is the same. The answer is: $\frac{19}{20}$

Permutations and Combinations

Factorials are products, indicated by an exclamation mark. For example, $4! = 4 \times 3 \times 2 \times 1$ (Remember that $0!$ is defined to be equal to 1)

- **Permutations:** The number of ways to choose a sample of k elements from a set of n distinct objects where order does matter, and replacements are not allowed. For a permutation problem, use this formula:

$$_nP_k = \frac{n!}{(n-k)!}$$

- **Combination:** The number of ways to choose a sample of r elements from a set of n distinct objects where order does not matter, and replacements are not allowed. For a combination problem, use this formula:

$$_nC_r = \frac{n!}{r!\,(n-r)!}$$

Examples:

Example 1. How many ways can the first and second place be awarded to 7 people?

Solution: Since the order matters, (the first and second place are different!) we need to use permutation formula where n is 7 and k is 2. Then: $\frac{n!}{(n-k)!} = \frac{7!}{(7-2)!} = \frac{7!}{5!} = \frac{7 \times 6 \times 5!}{5!}$, remove $5!$ from both sides of the fraction. Then: $\frac{7 \times 6 \times 5!}{5!} = 7 \times 6 = 42$

Example 2. How many ways can we pick a team of 3 people from a group of 8?

Solution: Since the order doesn't matter, we need to use a combination formula where n is 8 and r is 3.
Then: $\frac{n!}{r!\,(n-r)!} = \frac{8!}{3!\,(8-3)!} = \frac{8!}{3!\,(5)!} = \frac{8 \times 7 \times 6 \times 5!}{3!\,(5)!} = \frac{8 \times 7 \times 6}{3 \times 2 \times 1} = \frac{336}{6} = 56$

Chapter 12: Practices

✍ Find the values of the Given Data.

1) 6, 11, 5, 3, 6

Mode: _____   Range: _____

Mean: _____   Median: _____

2) 4, 9, 1, 9, 6, 7

Mode: _____   Range: _____

Mean: _____   Median: _____

3) 10, 3, 6, 10, 4, 15

Mode: _____   Range: _____

Mean: _____   Median: _____

4) 12, 4, 8, 9, 3, 12, 15

Mode: _____   Range: _____

Mean: _____   Median: _____

✍ The circle graph below shows all Bob's expenses for last month. Bob spent $790 on his Rent last month.

5) How much did Bob's total expenses last month? _____

6) How much did Bob spend for foods last month? _____

7) How much did Bob spend for his bills last month? _____

8) How much did Bob spend on his car last month? _____

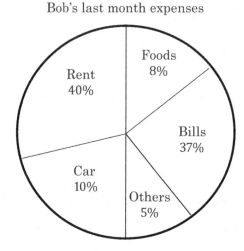

Bob's last month expenses

✎ Solve.

9) Bag A contains 8 red marbles and 6 green marbles. Bag B contains 5 black marbles and 7 orange marbles. What is the probability of selecting a green marble at random from bag A? What is the probability of selecting a black marble at random from Bag B?

_____   _____

✎ Solve.

10) Susan is baking cookies. She uses sugar, flour, butter, and eggs. How many different orders of ingredients can she try? _____

11) Jason is planning for his vacation. He wants to go to museum, go to the beach, and play volleyball. How many different ways of ordering are there for him? _____

12) In how many ways can a team of 6 basketball players choose a captain and co-captain? _____

13) How many ways can you give 5 balls to your 8 friends? _____

14) A professor is going to arrange her 5 students in a straight line. In how many ways can she do this? _____

15) In how many ways can a teacher chooses 12 out of 15 students?

_____

Effortless Math Education

Chapter 12: Answers

1) Mode: 6, Range: 8, Mean: 6.2, Median: 6

2) Mode: 9, Range:8, Mean: 6, Median: 6.5

3) Mode: 10, Range: 12, Mean: 8, Median: 8

4) Mode: 12, Range: 12, Mean: 9, Median: 9

5) $1,975

6) $158

7) $730.75

8) $197.50

9) $\frac{3}{7}, \frac{5}{12}$

10) 24

11) 6

12) 30 (it's a permutation problem)

13) 56 (it's a combination problem)

14) 120

15) 455 (it's a combination problem)

13 Functions Operations

Math topics that you'll learn in this chapter:

- ☑ Function Notation and Evaluation
- ☑ Adding and Subtracting Functions
- ☑ Multiplying and Dividing Functions
- ☑ Composition of Functions
- ☑ Function Inverses

123

Function Notation and Evaluation

- Functions are mathematical operations that assign unique outputs to given inputs.

- Function notation is the way a function is written. It is meant to be a precise way of giving information about the function without a rather lengthy written explanation.

- The most popular function notation is $f(x)$ which is read "f of x". Any letter can name a function. for example: $g(x)$, $h(x)$, etc.

- To evaluate a function, plug in the input (the given value or expression) for the function's variable (place holder, x).

Examples:

Example 1. Evaluate: $f(x) = x + 6$, find $f(2)$

Solution: Substitute x with 2:
Then: $f(x) = x + 6 \rightarrow f(2) = 2 + 6 \rightarrow f(2) = 8$

Example 2. Evaluate: $w(x) = 3x - 1$, find $w(4)$.

Solution: Substitute x with 4:
Then: $w(x) = 3x - 1 \rightarrow w(4) = 3(4) - 1 = 12 - 1 = 11$

Example 3. Evaluate: $f(x) = 2x^2 + 4$, find $f(-1)$.

Solution: Substitute x with -1:
Then: $f(x) = 2x^2 + 4 \rightarrow f(-1) = 2(-1)^2 + 4 \rightarrow f(-1) = 2 + 4 = 6$

Example 4. Evaluate: $h(x) = 4x^2 - 9$, find $h(2a)$.

Solution: Substitute x with $3a$:
Then: $h(x) = 4x^2 - 9 \rightarrow h(2a) = 4(2a)^2 - 9 \rightarrow h(2a) = 4(4a^2) - 9 = 16a^2 - 9$

bit.ly/3mls7lF

Find more at

Adding and Subtracting Functions

- Just like we can add and subtract numbers and expressions, we can add or subtract two functions and simplify or evaluate them. The result is a new function.

- For two functions $f(x)$ and $g(x)$, we can create two new functions:

$$(f + g)(x) = f(x) + g(x) \text{ and } (f - g)(x) = f(x) - g(x)$$

Examples:

Example 1. $g(x) = 2x - 2$, $f(x) = x + 1$, Find: $(g + f)(x)$

Solution: $(g + f)(x) = g(x) + f(x)$
Then: $(g + f)(x) = (2x - 2) + (x + 1) = 2x - 2 + x + 1 = 3x - 1$

Example 2. $f(x) = 4x - 3$, $g(x) = 2x - 4$, Find: $(f - g)(x)$

Solution: $(f - g)(x) = f(x) - g(x)$
Then: $(f - g)(x) = (4x - 3) - (2x - 4) = 4x - 3 - 2x + 4 = 2x + 1$

Example 3. $g(x) = x^2 + 2$, $f(x) = x + 5$, Find: $(g + f)(x)$

Solution: $(g + f)(x) = g(x) + f(x)$
Then: $(g + f)(x) = (x^2 + 2) + (x + 5) = x^2 + x + 7$

Example 4. $f(x) = 5x^2 - 3$, $g(x) = 3x + 6$, Find: $(f - g)(3)$

Solution: $(f - g)(x) = f(x) - g(x)$
Then: $(f - g)(x) = (5x^2 - 3) - (3x + 6) = 5x^2 - 3 - 3x - 6 = 5x^2 - 3x - 9$
Substitute x with 3: $(f - g)(3) = 5(3)^2 - 3(3) - 9 = 45 - 9 - 9 = 27$

bit.ly/3hdeFVO

Find more at

Multiplying and Dividing Functions

- Just like we can multiply and divide numbers and expressions, we can multiply and divide two functions and simplify or evaluate them.

- For two functions $f(x)$ and $g(x)$, we can create two new functions:

$$(f.g)(x) = f(x).g(x) \text{ and } \left(\frac{f}{g}\right)(x) = \frac{f(x)}{g(x)}$$

Examples:

Example 1. $g(x) = x + 3$, $f(x) = x + 4$, Find: $(g.f)(x)$

Solution:

$$(g.f)(x) = g(x).f(x) = (x+3)(x+4) = x^2 + 4x + 3x + 12 = x^2 + 7x + 12$$

Example 2. $f(x) = x + 6$, $h(x) = x - 9$, Find: $\left(\frac{f}{h}\right)(x)$

Solution: $\left(\frac{f}{h}\right)(x) = \frac{f(x)}{h(x)} = \frac{x+6}{x-9}$

Example 3. $g(x) = x + 7$, $f(x) = x - 3$, Find: $(g.f)(2)$

Solution:$(g.f)(x) = g(x).f(x) = (x+7)(x-3) = x^2 - 3x + 7x - 21$ $g(x).f(x) = x^2 + 4x - 21$

Substitute x with 2: $(g.f)(x) = (2)^2 + 4(2) - 21 = 4 + 8 - 21 = -9$

Example 4. $f(x) = x + 3$, $h(x) = 2x - 4$, Find: $\left(\frac{f}{h}\right)(3)$

Solution: $\left(\frac{f}{h}\right)(x) = \frac{f(x)}{h(x)} = \frac{x+3}{2x-4}$

Substitute x with 3: $\left(\frac{f}{h}\right)(x) = \frac{x+3}{2x-4} = \frac{3+3}{2(3)-4} = \frac{6}{2} = 3$

bit.ly/3ph7kHA

Find more at

Composition of Functions

- "Composition of functions" simply means combining two or more functions in a way where the output from one function becomes the input for the next function.

- The notation used for composition is: $(fog)(x) = f(g(x))$ and is read

  "f composed with g of x" or "f of g of x".

Examples:

Example 1. Using $f(x) = 2x + 3$ and $g(x) = 5x$, find: $(fog)(x)$

Solution: $(fog)(x) = f(g(x))$. Then: $(fog)(x) = f(g(x)) = f(5x)$

Now find $f(5x)$ by substituting x with $5x$ in $f(x)$ function.

Then: $f(x) = 2x + 3$; $(x \to 5x) \to f(5x) = 2(5x) + 3 = 10x + 3$

Example 2. Using $f(x) = 3x - 1$ and $g(x) = 2x - 2$, find: $(gof)(5)$

Solution: $(fog)(x) = f(g(x))$. Then: $(gof)(x) = g(f(x)) = g(3x - 1)$,

Now substitute x in $g(x)$ by $(3x - 1)$.

Then: $g(3x - 1) = 2(3x - 1) - 2 = 6x - 2 - 2 = 6x - 4$

Substitute x with 5: $(gof)(5) = g(f(x)) = 6x - 4 = 6(5) - 4 = 26$

Example 3. Using $f(x) = 2x^2 - 5$ and $g(x) = x + 3$, find: $f(g(3))$

Solution: First, find $g(3)$: $g(x) = x + 3 \to g(3) = 3 + 3 = 6$

Then: $f(g(3)) = f(6)$. Now, find $f(6)$ by substituting x with 6 in $f(x)$ function.

$f(g(3)) = f(6) = 2(6)^2 - 5 = 2(36) - 5 = 67$

Function Inverses

- An inverse function is a function that reverses another function: if the function f applied to an input x gives a result of y, then applying its inverse function g to y gives the result x. $f(x) = y$ if and only if $g(y) = x$

- The inverse function of $f(x)$ is usually shown by $f^{-1}(x)$.

Examples:

Example 1. Find the inverse of the function: $f(x) = 2x - 1$

Solution: First, replace $f(x)$ with y: $y = 2x - 1$, Then, replace all x's with y and all y's with x: $x = 2y - 1$, Now, solve for y: $x = 2y - 1 \rightarrow x + 1 = 2y \rightarrow \frac{1}{2}x + \frac{1}{2} = y$ Finally replace y with $f^{-1}(x)$: $f^{-1}(x) = \frac{1}{2}x + \frac{1}{2}$

Example 2. Find the inverse of the function: $g(x) = \frac{1}{5}x + 3$

Solution: $g(x) = \frac{1}{5}x + 3 \rightarrow y = \frac{1}{5}x + 3 \rightarrow$ replace all x's with y and all y's with x

$x = \frac{1}{5}y + 3$, solve for y: $\rightarrow x - 3 = \frac{1}{5}y \rightarrow 5(x - 3) = y \rightarrow y = 5x - 15 \rightarrow$

$$g^{-1}(x) = 5x - 15$$

Example 3. Find the inverse of the function: $h(x) = \sqrt{x} + 6$

Solution: $h(x) = \sqrt{x} + 6 \rightarrow y = \sqrt{x} + 6$, replace all x's with y and all y's with x

$\rightarrow x = \sqrt{y} + 6 \rightarrow x - 6 = \sqrt{y} \rightarrow (x - 6)^2 = (\sqrt{y})^2 \rightarrow x^2 - 12x + 36 = y$

$\rightarrow h^{-1}(x) = x^2 - 12x + 36$

bit.ly/3fmumtj

Find more at

Chapter 13: Practices

✍ Evaluate each function.

1) $g(n) = 2n + 5$, find $g(2)$

_____

2) $h(x) = 5x - 9$, find $h(4)$

_____

3) $k(n) = 10 - 6n$, find $k(2)$

_____

4) $g(x) = -5x + 6$, find $g(-2)$

_____

5) $k(n) = -8n + 3$, find $k(-6)$

_____

6) $w(n) = -2n - 9$, find $w(-5)$

_____

✍ Perform the indicated operation.

7) $f(x) = x + 6$
   $g(x) = 3x + 2$
   Find $(f - g)(x)$

_____

8) $g(x) = x - 9$
   $f(x) = 2x - 1$
   Find $(g - f)(x)$

_____

9) $h(t) = 5t + 6$
   $g(t) = 2t + 4$
   Find $(h + g)(x)$

_____

10) $g(a) = -6a + 1$
    $f(a) = 3a^2 - 3$
    Find $(g + f)(5)$

_____

11) $g(x) = 7x - 1$
    $h(x) = -4x^2 + 2$
    Find $(g - h)(-3)$

_____

12) $h(x) = -x^2 - 1$
    $g(x) = -7x - 1$
    Find $(h - g)(-5)$

_____

Effortless
Math
Education

✎ Perform the indicated operation.

13) $g(x) = x + 3$

      $f(x) = x + 1$

      Find $(g \cdot f)(x)$

      _____

14) $f(x) = 4x$

      $h(x) = x - 6$

      Find $(f \cdot h)(x)$

      _____

15) $g(a) = a - 8$

      $h(a) = 4a - 2$

      Find $(g \cdot h)(3)$

      _____

16) $f(x) = 6x + 2$

      $h(x) = 5x - 1$

      Find $\left(\frac{f}{h}\right)(-2)$

      _____

17) $f(x) = 7a - 1$

      $g(x) = -5 - 2a$

      Find $\left(\frac{f}{g}\right)(-4)$

      _____

18) $g(a) = a^2 - 4$

      $f(a) = a + 6$

      Find $\left(\frac{g}{f}\right)(-3)$

      _____

✎ Using $f(x) = 4x + 3$ and $g(x) = x - 7$, find:

19) $g\big(f(2)\big) =$ _____

20) $g\big(f(-2)\big) =$ _____

21) $f\big(g(4)\big) =$ _____

22) $f\big(f(7)\big) =$ _____

23) $g\big(f(5)\big) =$ _____

24) $g\big(f(-5)\big) =$ _____

✎ Find the inverse of each function.

25) $f(x) = \frac{1}{x} - 6 \rightarrow f^{-1}(x) =$

26) $g(x) = \frac{7}{-x-3} \rightarrow g^{-1}(x) =$

27) $h(x) = \frac{x+9}{3} \rightarrow h^{-1}(x) =$

28) $h(x) = \frac{2x-10}{4} \rightarrow h^{-1}(x) =$

29) $f(x) = \frac{-15+x}{3} \rightarrow f^{-1}(x) =$

30) $s(x) = \sqrt{x} - 2 \rightarrow s^{-1}(x) =$

Effortless
Math
Education

Effortless
Math
Education

Chapter 13: Answers

1) 9

2) 11

3) −2

4) 16

5) 51

6) 1

7) $-2x + 4$

8) $-x - 8$

9) $7t + 10$

10) 43

11) 12

12) −60

13) $x^2 + 4x + 3$

14) $4x^2 - 24x$

15) −50

16) $\frac{10}{11}$

17) $-\frac{29}{3}$

18) $\frac{5}{3}$

19) 4

20) −12

21) −9

22) 127

23) 16

24) −24

25) $f^{-1}(x) = \frac{1}{x+6}$

26) $g^{-1}(x) = -\frac{7+3x}{x}$

27) $h^{-1}(x) = 3x - 9$

28) $h^{-1}(x) = 2x + 5$

29) $f^{-1}(x) = 3x + 15$

30) $s^{-1}(x) = x^2 + 4x + 4$

CHAPTER

14 Quadratic

Math topics that you'll learn in this chapter:

- ☑ Solving a Quadratic Equation
- ☑ Graphing Quadratic Functions
- ☑ Solving Quadratic Inequalities
- ☑ Graphing Quadratic Inequalities

133

Solving a Quadratic Equation

- Write the equation in the form of: $ax^2 + bx + c = 0$

- Factorize the quadratic, set each factor equal to zero and solve.

- Use quadratic formula if you couldn't factorize the quadratic.

- Quadratic formula: $x = \frac{-b \pm \sqrt{b^2 - 4ac}}{2a}$

Examples:

Find the solutions of each quadratic function.

Example 1. $x^2 + 7x + 12 = 0$

Solution: Factor the quadratic by grouping. We need to find two numbers whose sum is 7 (from $7x$) and whose product is 12. Those numbers are 3 and 4. Then: $x^2 + 7x + 12 = 0 \rightarrow x^2 + 3x + 4x + 12 = 0 \rightarrow (x^2 + 3x) + (4x + 12) = 0$, Now, find common factors: $(x^2 + 3x) = x(x + 3)$ and $(4x + 12) = 3(x + 4)$. We have two expressions $(x^2 + 3x)$ and $(4x + 12)$ and their common factor is $(x + 3)$. Then: $(x^2 + 3x) + (4x + 12) = 0 \rightarrow x(x + 3) + 4(x + 3) = 0 \rightarrow (x + 3)(x + 4) = 0$.
The product of two expressions is 0. Then:
$(x + 3) = 0 \rightarrow x = -3$ or $(x + 4) = 0 \rightarrow x = -4$

Example 2. $x^2 + 5x + 6 = 0$

Solution: Use quadratic formula: $x_{1,2} = \frac{-b \pm \sqrt{b^2 - 4ac}}{2a}$, $a = 1, b = 5$ and $c = 6$
THEN: $x = \frac{-5 \pm \sqrt{5^2 - 4 \times 1(6)}}{2(1)}$, $x_1 = \frac{-5 + \sqrt{5^2 - 4 \times 1(6)}}{2(1)} = -2$, $x_2 = \frac{-5 - \sqrt{5^2 - 4 \times 1(6)}}{2(1)} = -3$

Graphing Quadratic Functions

- Quadratic functions in vertex form: $y = a(x - h)^2 + k$ where (h, k) is the vertex of the function. The axis of symmetry is $x = h$

- Quadratic functions in standard form: $y = ax^2 + bx + c$ where $x = -\frac{b}{2a}$ is the value of x in the vertex of the function.

- To graph a quadratic function, first find the vertex, then substitute some values for x and solve for y. (Remember that the graph of a quadratic function is a U-shaped curve and it is called "parabola".)

Example:

Sketch the graph of $y = (x + 2)^2 - 3$

Solution: Quadratic functions in vertex form: $y = a(x - h)^2 + k$ and (h, k) is the vertex. Then, the vertex of $y = (x + 2)^2 - 3$ is $(-2, -3)$.

Substitute zero for x and solve for y:
$y = (0 + 2)^2 - 3 = 1$.
The y Intercept is $(0,1)$.

Now, you can simply graph the quadratic function. Notice that quadratic function is a U-shaped curve.

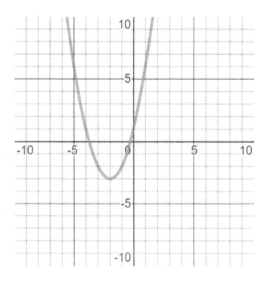

Solving Quadratic Inequalities

- A quadratic inequality is one that can be written in the standard form of

$ax^2 + bx + c > 0$ (or substitute $<, \le,$ or $\ge$ for $>$).

- Solving a quadratic inequality is like solving equations. We need to find the solutions (the zeroes).

- To solve quadratic inequalities, first find quadratic equations. Then choose a test value between zeroes. Finally, find interval(s), such as > 0 or < 0.

Examples:

Example 1. Solve quadratic inequality. $x^2 + x - 6 > 0$

Solution: First solve $x^2 + x - 6 = 0$ by factoring. Then: $x^2 + x - 6 = 0 \rightarrow$ $(x - 2)(x + 3) = 0$. The product of two expressions is 0. Then: $(x - 2) = 0 \rightarrow x = 2$ or $(x + 3) = 0 \rightarrow x = -3$. Now, choose a value between 2 and -3. Let's choose 0. Then: $x = 0 \rightarrow x^2 + x - 6 > 0 \rightarrow (0)^2 + (0) - 6 > 0 \rightarrow -6 > 0$

-6 is not greater than 0. Therefore, all values between 2 and -3 are NOT the solution of this quadratic inequality. The solution is: $x > 2$ and $x < -3$. To represent the solution, we can use interval notation, in which solution sets are indicated with parentheses or brackets. The solutions $x > 2$ and $x < -3$ represented as: $(\infty, -3) \cup (2, \infty)$

Example 2. Solve quadratic inequality. $x^2 - 2x - 8 \ge 0$

Solution: First solve: $x^2 - 2x - 8 = 0$, Factor: $x^2 - 2x - 8 = 0 \rightarrow$ $(x - 4)(x + 2) = 0$.

-2 and 4 are the solutions. Choose a point between -2 and 4. Let's choose 0. Then: $x = 0 \rightarrow x^2 - 2x - 8 \ge 0 \rightarrow (0)^2 - 2(0) - 8 \ge 0 \rightarrow -8 \ge 0$.

This is NOT true. So, the solution is: $x \le -2$ or $x \ge 4$ (using interval notation the solution is: $(\infty, -2] \cup [4, \infty)$

Graphing Quadratic Inequalities

- A quadratic inequality is in the form

$y > ax^2 + bx + c$ (or substitute $<, \leq$, or $\geq$ for $>$).

- To graph a quadratic inequality, start by graphing the quadratic parabola. Then fill in the region either inside or outside of it, depending on the inequality.

- Choose a testing point and check the solution section.

Example:

Sketch the graph of $y = 2x^2$

Solution: First, graph the quadratic $y = 2x^2$
Since the inequality sing is $>$, we need to use dash lines.

Now, choose a testing point inside the parabola. Let's choose (0,2).

$y > 2x^2 \rightarrow 2 > 2(0)^2 \rightarrow 2 > 0$

This is true. So, inside the parabola is the solution section.

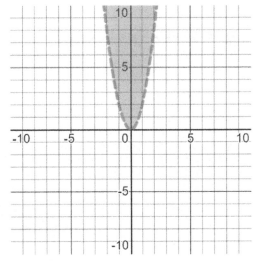

Chapter 14: Practices

✍ **Solve each equation by factoring or using the quadratic formula.**

1) $x^2 - 4x - 32 = 0$

_____

2) $x^2 - 2x - 63 = 0$

_____

3) $x^2 + 17x + 72 = 0$

_____

4) $x^2 + 14x + 48 = 0$

_____

5) $x^2 + 5x - 24 = 0$

_____

6) $x^2 + 15x + 36 = 0$

_____

✍ **Sketch the graph of each function.**

7) $y = (x + 1)^2 - 2$

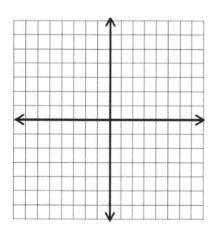

8) $y = (x - 1)^2 + 3$

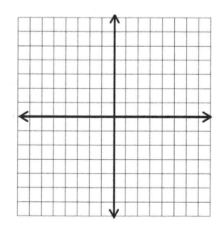

Effortless
Math
Education

✎ **Solve each quadratic inequality.**

9) $x^2 - 4 < 0$

_____

10) $x^2 - 9 > 0$

_____

11) $x^2 - 5x - 6 < 0$

_____

12) $x^2 + 8x - 20 > 0$

_____

13) $x^2 + 10x - 24 \geq 0$

_____

14) $x^2 + 17x + 72 \leq 0$

_____

✎ **Sketch the graph of each quadratic inequality.**

15) $y < -2x^2$

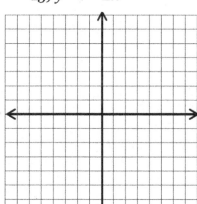

16) $y > 3x^2$

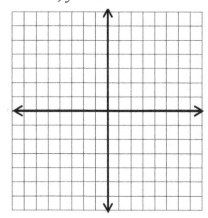

Chapter 14: Answers

1) $x^2 - 4x - 32 = 0$

$x = 8, x = -4$

2) $x^2 - 2x - 63 = 0$

$x = 9, x = -7$

3) $x^2 + 17x + 72 = 0$

$x = -9, x = -8$

4) $x^2 + 14x + 48 = 0$

$x = -6, x = -8$

5) $x^2 + 5x - 24 = 0$

$x = 3, x = -8$

6) $x^2 + 15x + 36 = 0$

$x = -12, x = -3$

7) $y = (x + 1)^2 - 2$

8) $y = (x - 1)^2 + 3$

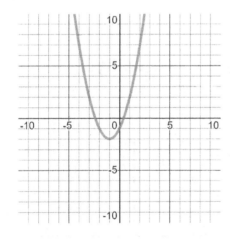

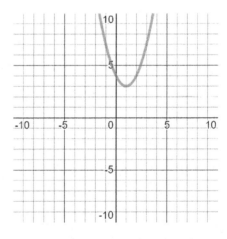

9) $x^2 - 4 < 0$

$-2 < x < 2$

10) $x^2 - 9 > 0$

$-3 < x < 3$

11) $x^2 - 5x - 6 < 0$

$-1 < x < 6$

12) $x^2 + 8x - 20 > 0$

$x < -10 \ or \ x > 2$

13) $x^2 + 10x - 24 \geq 0$

$x \leq -12 \ or \ x \geq 2$

14) $x^2 + 17x + 72 \leq 0$

$-9 \leq x \leq -8$

15) $y < -2x^2$ 16) $y > 3x^2$

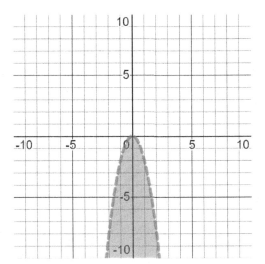   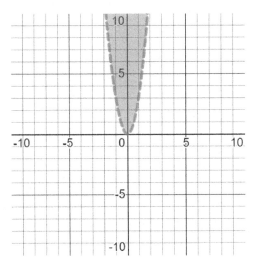

Effortless
Math
Education

15 Complex Numbers

Math topics that you'll learn in this chapter:

- ☑ Adding and Subtracting Complex Numbers
- ☑ Multiplying and Dividing Complex Numbers
- ☑ Rationalizing Imaginary Denominators

143

Adding and Subtracting Complex Numbers

- A complex number is expressed in the form $a + bi$, where a and b are real numbers, and i, which is called an imaginary number, is a solution of the equation $x^2 = -1$

- For adding complex numbers:

$$(a + bi) + (c + di) = (a + c) + (b + d)i$$

- For subtracting complex numbers:

$$(a + bi) - (c + di) = (a - c) + (b - d)i$$

Examples:

Example 1. Solve: $(8 + 4i) + (6 - 2i)$

Solution: Remove parentheses: $(8 + 4i) + (6 - 2i) = 8 + 4i + 6 - 2i$
Combine like terms: $8 + 4i + 6 - 2i = 14 + 2i$

Example 2. Solve: $(10 + 8i) + (8 - 3i)$

Solution: Remove parentheses: $(10 + 8i) + (8 - 3i) = 10 + 8i + 8 - 3i$
Group like terms: $10 + 8i + 8 - 3i = 18 + 5i$

Example 3. Solve: $(-5 - 3i) - (2 + 4i)$

Solution: Remove parentheses by multiplying -1 to the second parentheses:
$$(-5 - 3i) - (2 + 4i) = -5 - 3i - 2 - 4i$$
Combine like terms: $-5 - 3i - 2 - 4i = -7 - 7i$

Multiplying and Dividing Complex Numbers

- You can use FOIL (First-Out-In-Last) method or the following rule to multiply imaginary numbers. Remember that: $i^2 = -1$

$$(a + bi) + (c + di) = (ac - bd) + (ad + bc)i$$

- To divide complex numbers, you need to find the conjugate of the denominator. Conjugate of $(a + bi)$ is $(a - bi)$.

- Dividing complex numbers: $\dfrac{a+bi}{c+di} = \dfrac{a+bi}{c+di} \times \dfrac{c-di}{c-di} = \dfrac{ac+bd}{c^2+d^2} + \dfrac{bc-ad}{c^2+d^2}i$

Examples:

Example 1. Solve: $\dfrac{6-2i}{2+i}$

Solution: The conjugate of $(2 + i)$ is $(2 - i)$. Use the rule for dividing complex numbers:

$$\frac{a + bi}{c + di} = \frac{a + bi}{c + di} \times \frac{c - di}{c - di} = \frac{ac + bd}{c^2 + d^2} + \frac{bc - ad}{c^2 + d^2}i \rightarrow$$

$$\frac{6 - 2i}{2 + i} \times \frac{2 - i}{2 - i} = \frac{6 \times (2) + (-2)(1)}{2^2 + (1)^2} + \frac{-2 \times 2 - (6)(1)}{2^2 + (1)^2}i = \frac{10}{5} + \frac{-10}{5}i = 2 - 2i$$

Example 2. Solve: $(2 - 3i)(6 - 3i)$

Solution: Use the multiplication of imaginary numbers rule:

$$(a + bi) + (c + di) = (ac - bd) + (ad + bc)i$$
$$\big(2 \times 6 - (-3)(-3)\big) + (2(-3) + (-3) \times 6)i = 3 - 24i$$

Example 3. Solve: $\dfrac{3-2i}{4+i}$

Solution: Use the rule for dividing complex numbers: $\dfrac{a+bi}{c+di} = \dfrac{a+bi}{c+di} \times \dfrac{c-di}{c-di} =$

$$\frac{ac+bd}{c^2+d^2} + \frac{bc-ad}{c^2+d^2}i \rightarrow \frac{3-2i}{4+i} \times \frac{4-i}{4-i} = \frac{(3 \times 4 + (-2) \times 1) + (-2 \times 4 - 3 \times 1)i}{4^2 + 1^2} = \frac{10-11i}{17} = \frac{10}{17} - \frac{11}{17}i$$

Rationalizing Imaginary Denominators

- Step 1: Find the conjugate (it's the denominator with different sign between the two terms).

- Step 2: Multiply numerator and denominator by the conjugate.

- Step 3: Simplify if needed.

Examples:

Example 1. Solve: $\frac{4-3i}{6i}$

Solution: Multiply both numerator and denominator by $\frac{i}{i}$:

$$\frac{4-3i}{6i} = \frac{(4-3i)(i)}{6i(i)} = \frac{(4)(i)-(3i)(i)}{6(i^2)} = \frac{4i-3i^2}{6(-1)} = \frac{4i-3(-1)}{-6} = \frac{4i}{-6} + \frac{3}{-6} = -\frac{1}{2} - \frac{2}{3}i$$

Example 2. Solve: $\frac{6i}{2-i}$

Solution: Multiply both numerator and denominator by the conjugate

$\frac{2+i}{2+i}$: $\frac{6i(2+i)}{(2-i)(2+i)}$ = Apply complex arithmetic rule: $(a+bi)(a-bi) = a^2 + b^2$

$2^2 + (-1)^2 = 5$, then: $\frac{6i(2+i)}{(2-i)(2+i)} = \frac{-6+12i}{5} = -\frac{6}{5} + \frac{12}{5}i$

Example 3. Solve: $\frac{8-2i}{2i}$

Solution: Factor 2 from both sides: $\frac{8-2i}{2i} = \frac{2(4-i)}{2i}$, divide both sides by 2:

$\frac{2(4-i)}{2i} = \frac{(4-i)}{i}$

Multiply both numerator and denominator by $\frac{i}{i}$:

$$\frac{(4-i)}{i} = \frac{(4-i)}{i} \times \frac{i}{i} = \frac{(4i-i^2)}{i^2} = \frac{1+4i}{-1} = -1 - 4i$$

Chapter 15: Practices

✎ Evaluate.

1) $(-5i) - (7i) =$

2) $(-2i) + (-8i) =$

3) $(2i) - (6 + 3i) =$

4) $(4 - 6i) + (-2i) =$

5) $(-7i) + (4 + 5i) =$

6) $10 + (-2 - 6i) =$

7) $(-3i) - (9 + 2i) =$

8) $(4 + 6i) - (-3i) =$

✎ Calculate.

9) $(3 - 2i)(4 - 3i) =$

10) $(6 + 2i)(3 + 2i) =$

11) $(8 - i)(4 - 2i) =$

12) $(2 - 4i)(3 - 5i) =$

13) $(5 + 6i)(3 + 2i) =$

14) $(5 + 3i)(9 + 2i) =$

✎ Simplify.

15) $\frac{3}{2i} =$

16) $\frac{8}{-3i} =$

17) $\frac{-9}{2i} =$

18) $\frac{2-3i}{-5i} =$

19) $\frac{4-5i}{-2i} =$

20) $\frac{8+3i}{2i} =$

Answers – Chapter 15

1) $-12i$

2) $-10i$

3) $-6 - i$

4) $4 - 8i$

5) $4 - 2i$

6) $8 - 6i$

7) $-9 - 5i$

8) $4 + 9i$

9) $6 - 17i$

10) $14 + 18i$

11) $30 - 20i$

12) $-14 - 22i$

13) $3 + 28i$

14) $39 + 37i$

15) $-\dfrac{3i}{2}$

16) $\dfrac{8i}{3}$

17) $-\dfrac{9i}{2}$

18) $\dfrac{3}{5} + \dfrac{2}{5}i$

19) $\dfrac{5}{2} + 2i$

20) $\dfrac{3}{2} - 4i$

CHAPTER

16 Radicals

Math topics that you'll learn in this chapter:

- ☑ Simplifying Radical Expressions
- ☑ Adding and Subtracting Radical Expressions
- ☑ Multiplying Radical Expressions
- ☑ Rationalizing Radical Expressions
- ☑ Radical Equations
- ☑ Domain and Range of Radical Functions

149

Simplifying Radical Expressions

- Find the prime factors of the numbers or expressions inside the radical.

- Use radical properties to simplify the radical expression:

$$\sqrt[n]{x^a} = x^{\frac{a}{n}}, \sqrt[n]{xy} = x^{\frac{1}{n}} \times y^{\frac{1}{n}}, \sqrt[n]{\frac{x}{y}} = \frac{x^{\frac{1}{n}}}{y^{\frac{1}{n}}}, \text{ and } \sqrt[n]{x} \times \sqrt[n]{y} = \sqrt[n]{xy}$$

Examples:

Example 1. Find the square root of $\sqrt{144x^2}$.

Solution: Find the factor of the expression $144x^2$: $144 = 12 \times 12$ and $x^2 = x \times x$, now use radical rule: $\sqrt[n]{a^n} = a$, Then: $\sqrt{12^2} = 12$ and $\sqrt{x^2} = x$
Finally: $\sqrt{144x^2} = \sqrt{12^2} \times \sqrt{x^2} = 12 \times x = 12x$

Example 2. Write this radical in exponential form. $\sqrt[3]{x^4}$

Solution: To write a radical in exponential form, use this rule: $\sqrt[n]{x^a} = x^{\frac{a}{n}}$
Then: $\sqrt[3]{x^4} = x^{\frac{4}{3}}$

Example 3. Simplify. $\sqrt{8x^3}$

Solution: First factor the expression $8x^3$: $8x^3 = 2^3 \times x \times x \times x$, we need to find perfect squares: $8x^3 = 2^2 \times 2 \times x^2 \times x = 2^2 \times x^2 \times 2x$,
Then: $\sqrt{8x^3} = \sqrt{2^2 \times x^2} \times \sqrt{2x}$
Now use radical rule: $\sqrt[n]{a^n} = a$, Then: $\sqrt{2^2 \times x^2} \times \sqrt{(2x)} = 2x \times \sqrt{2x} = 2x\sqrt{2x}$

Example 4. Simplify. $\sqrt{27a^5b^4}$

Solution: First factor the expression $27a^5b^4$: $27a^5b^4 = 3^3 \times a^5 \times b^4$, we need to find perfect squares: $27a^5b^4 = 3^2 \times 3 \times a^4 \times a \times b^4$, Then:
$$\sqrt{27a^5b^4} = \sqrt{3^2 \times a^4 \times b^4} \times \sqrt{3a}$$
Now use radical rule: $\sqrt[n]{a^n} = a$, Then:
$$\sqrt{3^2 \times a^4 \times b^4} \times \sqrt{3a} = 3 \times a^2 \times b^2 \times \sqrt{3a} = 3a^2b^2\sqrt{3a}$$

Adding and Subtracting Radical Expressions

- Only numbers and expressions that have the same radical part can be added or subtracted.

- Remember, combining "unlike" radical terms is not possible.

- For numbers with the same radical part, just add or subtract factors outside the radicals.

Examples:

Example 1. Simplify: $8\sqrt{2} + 4\sqrt{2}$

Solution: Since we have the same radical parts, then we can add these two radicals: Add like terms: $8\sqrt{2} + 4\sqrt{2} = 12\sqrt{2}$

Example 2. Simplify: $11\sqrt{7} + 6\sqrt{7}$

Solution: Since we have the same radical parts, then we can add these two radicals: Add like terms: $11\sqrt{7} + 6\sqrt{7} = 17\sqrt{7}$

Example 3. Simplify: $2\sqrt{8} - 2\sqrt{2}$

Solution: The two radical parts are not the same. First, we need to simplify the $2\sqrt{8}$. Then: $2\sqrt{8} = 2\sqrt{4 \times 2} = 2(\sqrt{4})(\sqrt{2}) = 4\sqrt{2}$
Now, combine like terms: $2\sqrt{8} - 2\sqrt{2} = 4\sqrt{2} - 2\sqrt{2} = 2\sqrt{2}$

Example 4. Simplify: $5\sqrt{27} + 3\sqrt{3}$

Solution: The two radical parts are not the same. First, we need to simplify the $5\sqrt{27}$. Then: $5\sqrt{27} = 5\sqrt{9 \times 3} = 5(\sqrt{9})(\sqrt{3}) = 15\sqrt{3}$
Now, add: $5\sqrt{27} + 3\sqrt{3} = 15\sqrt{3} + 3\sqrt{3} = 18\sqrt{3}$

Multiplying Radical Expressions

To multiply radical expressions:

- Multiply the numbers and expressions outside of the radicals.

- Multiply the numbers and expressions inside the radicals.

- Simplify if needed.

Examples:

Example 1. Evaluate. $2\sqrt{5} \times \sqrt{3}$

Solution: Multiply the numbers outside of the radicals and the radical parts.
Then: $2\sqrt{5} \times \sqrt{3} = 2 \times 1 \times \sqrt{5} \times \sqrt{3} = 2\sqrt{15}$

Example 2. Multiply. $3x\sqrt{3} \times 4\sqrt{x}$

Solution: Multiply the numbers outside of the radicals and the radical parts.
Then, simplify: $3x\sqrt{3} \times 4\sqrt{x} = (3x \times 4) \times (\sqrt{3} \times \sqrt{x}) = (12x)(\sqrt{3x}) = 12x\sqrt{3x}$

Example 3. Evaluate. $5a\sqrt{5b} \times \sqrt{2b}$

Solution: Multiply the numbers outside of the radicals and the radical parts.
Then: $5a\sqrt{5b} \times \sqrt{2b} = 5a \times 1 \times \sqrt{5b} \times \sqrt{2b} = 5a\sqrt{10b^2}$
Simplify: $5a\sqrt{10b^2} = 5a \times \sqrt{10} \times \sqrt{b^2} = 5ab\sqrt{10}$

Example 4. Simplify. $11\sqrt{2x} \times 2\sqrt{8x}$

Solution: Multiply the numbers outside of the radicals and the radical parts.
Then, simplify: $11\sqrt{2x} \times 2\sqrt{8x} = (11 \times 2) \times (\sqrt{2x} \times \sqrt{8x}) = (22)(\sqrt{16x^2}) = 22\sqrt{16x^2}$
$\sqrt{16x^2} = 4x$, then: $22\sqrt{16x^2} = 22 \times 4x = 88x$

Rationalizing Radical Expressions

- Radical expressions cannot be in the denominator. (number in the bottom)

- To get rid of the radical in the denominator, multiply both numerator and denominator by the radical in the denominator.

- If there is a radical and another integer in the denominator, multiply both numerator and denominator by the conjugate of the denominator.

- The conjugate of $(a + b)$ is $(a - b)$ and vice versa.

Examples:

Example 1. Simplify $\frac{6}{\sqrt{2}}$

Solution: Multiply both numerator and denominator by $\sqrt{2}$. Then:

$\frac{6}{\sqrt{2}} \times \frac{\sqrt{2}}{\sqrt{2}} = \frac{6\sqrt{2}}{\sqrt{4}} = \frac{6\sqrt{2}}{2}$, Now, simplify: $\frac{6\sqrt{2}}{2} = 3\sqrt{2}$

Example 2. Simplify $\frac{5}{\sqrt{6} - 4}$

Solution: Multiply by the conjugate: $\frac{\sqrt{6} + 4}{\sqrt{6} + 4} \to \frac{5}{\sqrt{6} - 4} \times \frac{\sqrt{6} + 4}{\sqrt{6} + 4}$

$(\sqrt{6} - 4)(\sqrt{6} + 4) = -10$, then: $\frac{5}{\sqrt{6} - 4} \times \frac{\sqrt{6} + 4}{\sqrt{6} + 4} = \frac{5(\sqrt{6} + 4)}{-10}$

Use the fraction rule: $\frac{a}{-b} = -\frac{a}{b} \to \frac{5(\sqrt{6} + 4)}{-10} = -\frac{5(\sqrt{6} + 4)}{10} = -\frac{1}{2}(\sqrt{6} + 4)$

Example 3. Simplify $\frac{2}{\sqrt{3} - 1}$

Solution: Multiply by the conjugate: $\frac{\sqrt{3} + 1}{\sqrt{3} + 1}$

$\frac{2}{\sqrt{3} - 1} \times \frac{\sqrt{3} + 1}{\sqrt{3} + 1} = \frac{2(\sqrt{3} + 1)}{2} \to = (\sqrt{3} + 1)$

bit.ly/3vKudGO

Find more at

Radical Equations

To solve a radical equation:

- Isolate the radical on one side of the equation.

- Square both sides of the equation to remove the radical.

- Solve the equation for the variable.

- Plugin the answer (answers) into the original equation to avoid extraneous values.

Examples:

Example 1. Solve $\sqrt{x} - 5 = 15$

Solution: Add 5 to both sides: $\sqrt{x} = 20$

Square both sides:

$$\left(\sqrt{x}\right)^2 = 20^2 \rightarrow x = 400$$

Plugin the value of 400 for x in the original equation and check the answer:

$$x = 400 \rightarrow \sqrt{x} - 5 = \sqrt{400} - 5 = 20 - 5 = 15$$

So, the value of 400 for x is correct.

Example 2. What is the value of x in this equation?

$$2\sqrt{x + 1} = 4$$

Solution: Divide both sides by 2. Then:

$$2\sqrt{x + 1} = 4 \rightarrow \frac{2\sqrt{x + 1}}{2} = \frac{4}{2} \rightarrow \sqrt{x + 1} = 2$$

Square both sides: $\left(\sqrt{(x + 1)}\right)^2 = 2^2$, Then: $x + 1 = 4 \rightarrow x = 3$

Substitute x by 3 in the original equation and check the answer:

$$x = 3 \rightarrow 2\sqrt{x + 1} = 2\sqrt{3 + 1} = 2\sqrt{4} = 2(2) = 4$$

So, the value of 3 for x is correct.

Domain and Range of Radical Functions

- To find the domain of a radical function, find all possible values of the variable inside radical.

- Remember that having a negative number under the square root symbol is not possible. (For cubic roots, we can have negative numbers)

- To find the range, plugin the minimum and maximum values of the variable inside radical.

Examples:

Example 1. Find the domain and range of the radical function. $y = \sqrt{x - 3}$

Solution: For domain: Find non-negative values for radicals: $x - 3 \geq 0$

Domain of functions: $x - 3 \geq 0 \rightarrow x \geq 3$

Domain of the function $y = \sqrt{x - 3}$: $x \geq 3$

For range: The range of a radical function of the form $c\sqrt{ax + b} + k$ is: $f(x) \geq k$

For the function $y = \sqrt{x - 3}$, the value of k is 0. Then: $f(x) \geq 0$

Range of the function $y = \sqrt{x - 3}$: $f(x) \geq 0$

Example 2. Find the domain and range of the radical function. $y = 5\sqrt{3x + 6} + 4$

Solution: For domain: Find non-negative values for radicals: $3x + 6 \geq 0$

Domain of functions: $3x + 6 \geq 0 \rightarrow 3x \geq -6 \rightarrow x \geq -2$

Domain of the function $y = 5\sqrt{3x + 6} + 4$: $x \geq -2$

For range: The range of a radical function of the form $c\sqrt{ax + b} + k$ is: $f(x) \geq k$

For the function $y = 5\sqrt{3x + 6} + 4$, the value of k is 4. Then: $f(x) \geq 4$

Range of the function $y = 5\sqrt{3x + 6} + 4$: $f(x) \geq 4$

bit.ly/2Pn4vlj

Find more at

Chapter 16: Practices

✎ Simplify.

1) $\sqrt{256y} =$

2) $\sqrt{900} =$

3) $\sqrt{144a^2b} =$

4) $\sqrt{36 \times 9} =$

✎ Simplify.

5) $3\sqrt{5} + 2\sqrt{5} =$

6) $6\sqrt{3} + 4\sqrt{27} =$

7) $5\sqrt{2} + 10\sqrt{18} =$

8) $7\sqrt{2} - 5\sqrt{8} =$

✎ Evaluate.

9) $\sqrt{5} \times \sqrt{3} =$

10) $\sqrt{6} \times \sqrt{8} =$

11) $3\sqrt{5} \times \sqrt{9} =$

12) $2\sqrt{3} \times 3\sqrt{7} =$

✎ Simplify.

13) $\frac{1}{\sqrt{3}-6} =$

14) $\frac{5}{\sqrt{2}+7} =$

15) $\frac{\sqrt{3}}{1-\sqrt{6}} =$

16) $\frac{2}{\sqrt{3}+5} =$

✎ Solve for x.

17) $\sqrt{x} + 2 = 9$

18) $3 + \sqrt{x} = 12$

19) $\sqrt{x} + 5 = 30$

20) $\sqrt{x} - 9 = 27$

21) $10 = \sqrt{x+1}$

22) $\sqrt{x+4} = 3$

**Effortless
Math
Education**

Identify the domain and range of each function.

23) $y = \sqrt{x + 2} - 1$

25) $y = \sqrt{x - 4}$

24) $y = \sqrt{x + 1}$

26) $y = \sqrt{x - 3} + 1$

Effortless
Math
Education

Answers – Chapter 16

1) $16\sqrt{y}$

2) 30

3) $12a\sqrt{b}$

4) 18

5) $5\sqrt{5}$

6) $18\sqrt{3}$

7) $35\sqrt{2}$

8) $-3\sqrt{2}$

9) $\sqrt{15}$

10) $\sqrt{48} = 4\sqrt{3}$

11) $9\sqrt{5}$

12) $6\sqrt{21}$

13) $-\dfrac{\sqrt{3}+6}{33}$

14) $-\dfrac{5(\sqrt{2}-7)}{47}$

15) $-\dfrac{\sqrt{3}+3\sqrt{2}}{5}$

16) $-\dfrac{\sqrt{3}-5}{11}$

17) $x = 49$

18) $x = 81$

19) $x = 625$

20) $x = 1,296$

21) $x = 99$

22) $x = 5$

23) $x \geq -2, y \geq -1$

24) $x \geq -1, y \geq 0$

25) $x \geq 4, y \geq 0$

26) $x \geq 3, y \geq 1$

17 Logarithms

Math topics that you'll learn in this chapter:

- ☑ Evaluating Logarithms
- ☑ Expanding and Condensing Logarithms
- ☑ Natural Logarithm
- ☑ Solving Logarithmic Equations

159

Evaluating Logarithms

- Logarithm is another way of writing exponent. $log_b{}^y = x$ is equivalent to $y = b^x$.

- Learn some logarithms rules: ($a > 0, a \neq 0, M > 0, N > 0$, and k is a real number.)

Rule 1: $log_a(M.N) = log_aM + log_aN$ Rule 4: $log_aa = 1$

Rule 2: $log_a\dfrac{M}{N} = log_aM - log_aN$ Rule 5: $log_a{}^1 = 0$

Rule 3: $log_a(M)^k = klog_aM$ Rule 6: $a^{log_ak} = k$

Examples:

Example 1. Evaluate: $log_2 32$

Solution: Rewrite 32 in power base form: $32 = 2^5$, then: $log_2 32 = log_2(2^5)$

Use log rule: $log_a(M)^k = k.log_a(M) \rightarrow log_2(2^5) = 5log_2(2)$

Use log rule: $log_a(a) = 1 \rightarrow log_2(2) = 1.$ $5log_2(2) = 5 \times 1 = 5$

Example 2. Evaluate: $3log_5 125$

Solution: Rewrite 125 in power base form: $125 = 5^3$, then: $log_5 125 = log_5(5^3)$

Use log rule: $log_a(M)^k = k.log_a(M) \rightarrow log_5(5^3) = 3log_5(5)$

Use log rule: $log_a(a) = 1 \rightarrow log_5(5) = 1.$ $3 \times 3log_5(5) = 3 \times 3 = 9$

Example 3. Evaluate: $log_3 (3)^5$

Solution: Use log rule: $log_a(M)^k = k.log_a(M) \rightarrow log_3 (3)^5 = 5log_3(3)$

Use log rule: $log_a(a) = 1 \rightarrow log_3(3) = 1 \rightarrow 5 \times log_3(3) = 5 \times 1 = 5$

Expanding and Condensing Logarithms

- Using some of properties of logs, (the product rule, quotient rule, and power rule) sometimes we can expand a logarithm expression (expanding) or convert some logarithm expressions into a single logarithm (condensing).

- Let's review some logarithms properties:

$$a^{\log_a b} = b$$

$$\log_a \frac{1}{x} = -\log_a x$$

$$\log_a 1 = 0$$

$$\log_a x^p = p \, \log_a x$$

$$\log_a a = 1$$

$$\log_{x^k} x = \frac{1}{x} \, \log_a x, for \; k \neq 0$$

$$\log_a (x \cdot y) = \log_a x + \log_a y$$

$$\log_a x = \log_{a^c} x^c$$

$$\log_a \frac{x}{y} = \log_a x - \log_a y$$

$$\log_a x = \frac{1}{\log_x a}$$

Examples:

Example 1. Expand this logarithm. $\log_a (3 \times 5) =$

Solution: Use log rule: $\log_a(x \cdot y) = \log_a x + \log_a y$
Then: $\log_a (3 \times 5) = \log_a 3 + \log_a 5$

Example 2. Condense this expression to a single logarithm. $\log_a 2 - \log_a 7$

Solution: Use log rule: $\log_a x - \log_a y = \log_a \frac{x}{y}$
Then: $\log_a 2 - \log_a 7 = \log_a \frac{2}{7}$

Example 3. Expand this logarithm. $\log \left(\frac{1}{7}\right) =$

Solution: Use log rule: $\log_a \frac{1}{x} = -\log_a x$
Then: $\log \left(\frac{1}{7}\right) = -\log 7$

Natural Logarithms

- A natural logarithm is a logarithm that has a special base of the mathematical constant e, which is an irrational number approximately equal to 2.71.

- The natural logarithm of x is generally written as $ln\ x$, or $log_e\ x$.

Examples:

Example 1. Expand this natural logarithm. $ln\ 4x^2 =$

Solution: Use log rule: $log_a(x \cdot y) = log_a\ x + log_a\ y$
Then: $ln\ 4x^2 = ln\ 4 + ln\ x^2$. Now, use log rule: $log_a(M)^k = k.\ log_a(M) \rightarrow$
$$ln\ 4 + ln\ x^2 = ln\ 4 + 2\ ln\ x$$

Example 2. Condense this expression to a single logarithm. $ln\ x - log_e\ 2y$

Solution: Use log rule: $log_a\ x - log_a\ y = log_a\ \frac{x}{y}$

Then: $ln\ x - log_e\ 2y = ln\ \frac{x}{2y}$

Example 3. Solve this equation for x: $e^x = 6$

Solution: If $f(x) = g(x), then:\ ln(f(x)) = ln(g(x)) \rightarrow ln(e^x) = ln(6)$
Use log rule: $log_a\ x^b = b\ log_a\ x \rightarrow ln(e^x) = x\ ln(e) \rightarrow xln(e) = ln(6)$
$ln(e) = 1$, then: $x = ln(6)$

Example 4. Solve this equation for x: $ln(4x - 2) = 1$

Solution: Use log rule: $a = log_b(b^a) \rightarrow 1 = ln(e^1) = ln(e) \rightarrow ln(4x - 2) = ln\ (e)$
When the logs have the same base: $log_b\big(f(x)\big) = log_b\big(g(x)\big) \rightarrow f(x) = g(x)$
$$ln(4x - 2) = ln(e), \text{then: } 4x - 2 = e \rightarrow x = \frac{e+2}{4}$$

Solving Logarithmic Equations

To solve a logarithm equation:

- Convert the logarithmic equation to an exponential equation when it's possible. (If no base is indicated, the base of the logarithm is 10)

- Condense logarithms if you have more than one log on one side of the equation.

- Plug in the answers back into the original equation and check to see if the solution works.

Examples:

Example 1. Find the value of x in this equation. $\log_2(36 - x^2) = 4$

Solution: Use log rule: $\log_b x = \log_b y$, then: $x = y$
We can write number 4 as a logarithm: $4 = \log_2(2^4)$
Then: $\log_2(36 - x^2) = \log_2(2^4) = \log_2 16$
Then: $36 - x^2 = 16 \rightarrow 36 - 16 = x^2 \rightarrow x^2 = 20 \rightarrow x = \pm\sqrt{20} = \pm 2\sqrt{5}$
You can plug in back the solutions into the original equation to check your answer. $x = \sqrt{20} \rightarrow \log_2(36 - \sqrt{20}^2) = 4 \rightarrow \log_2(36 - 20) = 4 \rightarrow \log_2 16 = 4$
$\quad x = -\sqrt{20} \rightarrow \log_2(36 - (-\sqrt{20})^2) = 4 \rightarrow \log_2(36 - 20) = 4 \rightarrow \log_2 16 = 4$
Both solutions work in the original equation.

Example 2. Find the value of x in this equation. $\log(5x + 2) = \log(3x - 1)$

Solution: When the logs have the same base: $f(x) = g(x)$, *then*:
$\ln(f(x)) = \ln(g(x))$, $\log(5x + 2) = \log(3x - 1) \rightarrow 5x + 2 = 3x - 1 \rightarrow$
$$5x + 2 - 3x + 1 = 0 \rightarrow 2x + 3 = 0 \rightarrow 2x = -3 \rightarrow x = -\frac{3}{2}$$
Verify Solution: $\log(5x + 2) = \log\left(5\left(-\frac{3}{2}\right) + 2\right) = \log(-5.5)$

Logarithms of negative numbers are not defined. Therefore, there is no solution for this equation

Chapter 17: Practices

✎ **Expand each logarithm.**

1) $log_b(2 \times 9) =$

2) $log_b(5 \times 7) =$

3) $log_b(xy) =$

4) $log_b(2x^2 \times 3y) =$

✎ **Evaluate each logarithm.**

5) $2log_9(9) =$

6) $3log_2(8) =$

7) $2log_5(125) =$

8) $log_{100}(1) =$

9) $log_{10}(100) =$

10) $3log_4(16) =$

11) $\frac{1}{2}log_3(81) =$

12) $log_7(343) =$

✎ **Reduce the following expressions to simplest form.**

13) $e^{ln4+ln5} =$

14) $e^{ln\left(\frac{9}{e}\right)} =$

15) $e^{ln2+ln7} =$

16) $6\,ln(e^5) =$

✎ **Find the value of the variables in each equation.**

17) $log_3 8x = 3 \rightarrow x =$ ____

18) $log_4 2x = 5 \rightarrow x =$ ____

19) $log_4 5x = 0 \rightarrow x =$ ____

20) $log 4x = log 5 \rightarrow x =$ ____

Effortless

Math

Education

Answers – Chapter 17

1) $log_b 2 + 2 log_b 3$

2) $log_b 5 + log_b 7$

3) $log_b x + log_b y$

4) $log_b 2 + log_b x^2 + log_b 3 + log_b y$

5) 2

6) 9

7) 6

8) 0

9) 2

10) 6

11) 2

12) 3

13) 20

14) $\frac{9}{e}$

15) 14

16) 30

17) $\frac{27}{8}$

18) 512

19) $\frac{1}{5}$

20) $\frac{5}{4}$

CHAPTER

18 Circles

Math topics that you'll learn in this chapter:

- ☑ Circumference and Area of Circles
- ☑ Arc length and sector Area
- ☑ Equation of a Circle
- ☑ Finding the Center and the Radius of Circles

167

Circumference and Area of Circles

- In a circle, variable r is usually used for the radius and d for diameter.

- *Area of a circle* $= \pi r^2$ (π is about 3.14)

- *Circumference of a circle* $= 2\pi r$

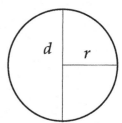

Examples:

Example 1. Find the area of this circle.

Solution:
Use area formula: $Area = \pi r^2$
$r = 8 \, in \rightarrow Area = \pi(8)^2 = 64\pi$, $\pi = 3.14$
Then: $Area = 64 \times 3.14 = 200.96 \, in^2$

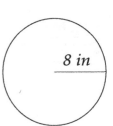

Example 2. Find the Circumference of this circle.

Solution:
Use Circumference formula: $Circumference = 2\pi r$
$r = 5 \, cm \rightarrow Circumference = 2\pi(5) = 10\pi$
$\pi = 3.14$ Then: $Circumference = 10 \times 3.14 = 31.4 \, cm$

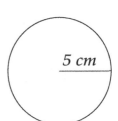

Example 3. Find the area of the circle.

Solution:
Use area formula: $Area = \pi r^2$,
$r = 5 \, in$, then: $Area = \pi(5)^2 = 25\pi$, $\pi = 3.14$
Then: $Area = 25 \times 3.14 = 78.5$

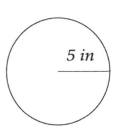

Arc Length and Sector Area

- To find the area of a sector of a circle, use this formula:

Area of a sector $= \pi r^2 (\frac{\theta}{360})$, r is the radius of the circle and θ is the central angle of the sector.

- To find the arc of a sector of a circle, use this formula:

Arc of a sector $= (\frac{\theta}{180}) \pi r$

Examples:

Example 1. Find the length of the arc. Round your answers to the nearest tenth.

$$(\pi = 3.14), r = 20 \; cm, \theta = 30°$$

Solution: Use this formula: Length of the sector $= \left(\frac{\theta}{180}\right) \pi r =$

$\left(\frac{30}{180}\right) \pi (20) = \left(\frac{1}{6}\right) \pi (20) = \left(\frac{20}{6}\right) \times 3.14 \cong 10.5 \; cm$

Example 2. Find the area of the sector. $(\pi = 3.14)$ r = 6 ft, $\theta = 70°$

Solution: Use this formula: area of a sector $= \pi r^2 (\frac{\theta}{360})$

Area of the sector $= \pi r^2 \left(\frac{\theta}{360}\right) = (3.14)(6^2) \left(\frac{70}{360}\right) = 21.98 \; ft^2$

Example 3. Find the length of the arc. $(\pi = 3.14)$ r = 3 ft, $\theta = \frac{\pi}{3}$

Solution: $\theta = \frac{\pi}{3} \rightarrow \frac{\pi}{3} \times \frac{180}{\pi} = 60°$

Length of the sector $= \left(\frac{60}{180}\right) \pi (3) = \left(\frac{1}{3}\right) \pi (3) = 1 \times 3.14 = 3.14 \; cm$

bit.ly/34WIWmZ
Find more at

Equation of a Circle

- Equation of circles in standard form: $(x - h)^2 + (y - k)^2 = r^2$

Center: (h, k), Radius: r

- Equation of circles in general form: $x^2 + y^2 + Ax + By + C = 0$

Examples:

Write the standard form equation of each circle.

Example 1. $x^2 + y^2 - 4x - 6y + 9 = 0$

Solution: The standard form of circle equation is: $(x - h)^2 + (y - k)^2 = r^2$ where the radius of the circle is r, and it's centered at (h, k).

First, move the loose number to the right side: $x^2 + y^2 - 4x - 6y = -9$

Group x-variables and y-variables together: $(x^2 - 4x) + (y^2 - 6y) = -9$

Convert x to square form:

$(x^2 - 4x + 4) + y^2 - 6y = -9 + 4 \to (x - 2)^2 + (y^2 - 6y) = -9 + 4$

Convert y to square form:

$(x - 2)^2 + (y^2 - 6y + 9) = -9 + 4 + 9 \to (x - 2)^2 + (y - 3)^2 = 4$

Then, the equation of the circle in standard form is: $(x - 2)^2 + (y - 3)^2 = 2^2$

Example 2. The center of the circle is at $(-2, -10)$, and its radius is 5.

Solution: $(x - h)^2 + (y - k)^2 = r^2$ is the circle equation with a radius r, centered at (h, k). So, $h = -2$, $k = -10$ and $r = 5$

Then, the equation of the circle is: $(x - (-2))^2 + (y - (-10))^2 = (5)^2$

Finding the Center and the Radius of Circles

To find the center and the radius of a circle using the equation of the circle:

- Write the equation of the circle in standard form: $(x - h)^2 + (y - k)^2 = r^2$,

- The center of the circle is at (h, k), and its radius is r.

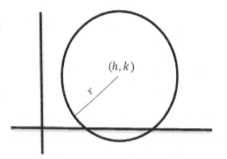

Examples:

Identify the center and the radius of each circle:

Example 1. $x^2 + y^2 - 4x + 3 = 0$

Solution: $(x - h)^2 + (y - k)^2 = r^2$ is the circle equation with a radius r, centered at (h, k).

Rewrite $x^2 + y^2 - 4x + 3 = 0$ in the standard form:

$x^2 + y^2 - 4x + 3 = 0 \rightarrow (x - 2)^2 + y^2 = 1^2$

Then, the center is at: $(2, 0)$ and $r = 1$

Example 2. $8x + x^2 + 10y = 8 - y^2$

Solution: Rewrite the equation in standard form:

$8x + x^2 + 10y = 8 - y^2 \rightarrow (x - (-4))^2 + (y - (-5))^2 = 7^2$

Then, the center is at $(-4, -5)$ and the radius is 7.

bit.ly/3tTV6as

Find more at

Chapter 18: Practices

✍ Complete the table below. ($\pi = 3.14$)

1)

	Radius	Diameter	Circumference	Area
Circle 1	3 inches	6 inches	18.84 inches	28.26 square inches
Circle 2			43.96 meters	
Circle 3		8 ft		
Circle 4				78.5 square miles

✍ Find the length of each arc. Round your answers to the nearest hundredth.

2) $r = 4$ cm, $\theta = 28° \rightarrow$ arc $=$

3) $r = 6$ ft, $\theta = 30° \rightarrow$ arc $=$

4) $r = 8$ ft, $\theta = 40° \rightarrow$ arc $=$

5) $r = 12$ cm, $\theta = 34° \rightarrow$ arc $=$

✍ Write the standard form equation of each circle.

6) $x^2 + y^2 - 4x + 2y - 4 = 0 \rightarrow$

7) $x^2 + y^2 - 8x + 6y - 11 = 0 \rightarrow$

8) $x^2 + y^2 - 10x - 12y + 12 = 0 \rightarrow$

9) $x^2 + y^2 + 12x - 6y - 19 = 0 \rightarrow$

10) $x^2 + y^2 - 6x + 8y + 24 = 0 \rightarrow$

✍ Identify the center and radius of each circle.

11) $(x + 1)^2 + (y - 2)^2 = 5 \rightarrow$ Center: (___,___) Radius: _____

12) $(x - 5)^2 + (y + 10)^2 = 4 \rightarrow$ Center: (___,___) Radius: _____

13) $x^2 + (y - 3)^2 = 8 \rightarrow$ Center: (___,___) Radius: _____

14) $(x - 1)^2 + y^2 = 9 \rightarrow$ Center: (___,___) Radius: _____

15) $x^2 + y^2 = 16 \rightarrow$ Center: (___,___) Radius: _____

16) $(x + 1)^2 + (y + 6)^2 = 10 \rightarrow$ Center: (___,___) Radius: _____

Effortless
Math
Education

Answers – Chapter 18

1)	Radius	Diameter	Circumference	Area
Circle 1	3 inches	6 inches	18.84 inches	28.26 square inches
Circle 2	7 meters	14 meters	43.96 meters	153.86 square meters
Circle 3	4 ft	8 ft	25.12 ft	50.24 square ft
Circle 4	5 miles	10 miles	31.4 miles	78.5 square miles

2) $1.95 \ cm$

3) $3.14 \ ft$

4) $5.58 \ ft$

5) $7.12 \ cm$

6) $(x-2)^2 + (y-(-1))^2 = 3^2$

7) $(x-4)^2 + (y-(-3))^2 = 6^2$

8) $(x-5)^2 + (y-6)^2 = 7^2$

9) $(x-(-6))^2 + (y-3)^2 = 8^2$

10) $(x-3)^2 + (y-(-4))^2 = 1^2$

11)   Center: $(-1, 2)$, Radius: $\sqrt{5}$

12)   Center: $(5, -10)$, Radius: 2

13)   Center: $(0, 3)$, Radius: $2\sqrt{2}$

14)   Center: $(1, 0)$, Radius: 3

15)   Center: $(0, 0)$, Radius: 4

16)   Center: $(-1, -6)$, Radius: $\sqrt{10}$

Effortless Math Education

CHAPTER

19 Rational Expressions

Math topics that you'll learn in this chapter:

- ☑ Simplifying Complex Fractions
- ☑ Graphing Rational Expressions
- ☑ Adding and Subtracting Rational Expressions
- ☑ Multiplying Rational Expressions
- ☑ Dividing Rational Expressions
- ☑ Rational Equations

175

Simplifying Complex Fractions

- Convert mixed numbers to improper fractions.

- Simplify all fractions.

- Write the fraction in the numerator of the main fraction line then write division sign ($\div$) and the fraction of the denominator.

- Use normal method for dividing fractions.

- Simplify as needed.

Examples:

Example 1. Simplify: $\dfrac{\frac{3}{5}}{\frac{2}{25}-\frac{5}{16}}$

Solution: First, simplify the denominator: $\dfrac{2}{25}-\dfrac{5}{16}=-\dfrac{93}{400}$,

Then: $\dfrac{\frac{3}{5}}{\frac{2}{25}-\frac{5}{16}}=\dfrac{\frac{3}{5}}{-\frac{93}{400}}$; Now, write the complex fraction using the division sign:

$\dfrac{\frac{3}{5}}{\frac{93}{400}}=\dfrac{3}{5}\div\left(-\dfrac{93}{400}\right)$. Use the dividing fractions rule: Keep, Change, Flip (keep the first fraction, change the division sign to multiplication, flip the second fraction)

$$\frac{3}{5}\div\left(-\frac{93}{400}\right)=\frac{3}{5}\times\frac{400}{93}=-\frac{240}{93}=-\frac{80}{31}=2\frac{18}{31}$$

Example 2. Simplify: $\dfrac{\frac{2}{5}\div\frac{1}{3}}{\frac{5}{9}+\frac{1}{3}}$

Solution: First, simplify the numerator: $\dfrac{2}{5}\div\dfrac{1}{3}=\dfrac{6}{5}$, then, simplify the denominator: $\dfrac{5}{9}+\dfrac{1}{3}=\dfrac{8}{9}$, Now, write the complex fraction using the division sign ($\div$): $\dfrac{\frac{2}{5}\div\frac{1}{3}}{\frac{5}{9}+\frac{1}{3}}=\dfrac{\frac{6}{5}}{\frac{8}{9}}=\dfrac{6}{5}\div\dfrac{8}{9}$, Use the dividing fractions rule: (Keep, Change, Flip) $\dfrac{6}{5}\div\dfrac{8}{9}=\dfrac{6}{5}\times\dfrac{9}{8}=\dfrac{54}{40}=\dfrac{27}{20}=1\dfrac{7}{20}$

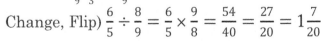

Graphing Rational Expressions

- A rational expression is a fraction in which the numerator and/or the denominator are polynomials. Examples: $\frac{1}{x}, \frac{x^2}{x-1}, \frac{x^2-x+2}{x^2+5x+1}, \frac{m^2+6m-5}{m-2m}$
- To graph a rational function:

  o Find the vertical asymptotes of the function if there is any. (Vertical asymptotes are vertical lines which correspond to the zeroes of the denominator. The graph will have a vertical asymptote at $x = a$ if the denominator is zero at $x = a$ and the numerator isn't zero at $x = a$)

  o Find the horizontal or slant asymptote. (If the numerator has a bigger degree than the denominator, there will be a slant asymptote. To find the slant asymptote, divide the numerator by the denominator using either long division or synthetic division.)

  o If the denominator has a bigger degree than the numerator, the horizontal asymptote is the x-axes or the line $y = 0$. If they have the same degree, the horizontal asymptote equals the leading coefficient (the coefficient of the largest exponent) of the numerator divided by the leading coefficient of the denominator.

  o Find intercepts and plug in some values of x and solve for y, then graph the function.

Example:

Graph rational function. $f(x) = \frac{x^2-x+2}{x-1}$

Solution: First, notice that the graph is in two pieces. Most rational functions have graphs in multiple pieces. Find $y - intercept$ by substituting zero for x and solving for y ($f(x)$): $x = 0 \rightarrow y = \frac{x^2-x+2}{x-1} = \frac{0^2-0+2}{0-1} = -2$,

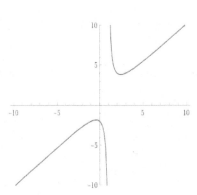

$$y - intercept: (0, -2)$$

Asymptotes of $\frac{x^2-x+2}{x-1}$: Vertical: $x = 1$, Slant asymptote:

$y = 2x + 1$ (divide the numerator by the denominator). After finding the asymptotes, you can plug in some values for x and solve for y. Here is the sketch for this function.

Adding and Subtracting Rational Expressions

For adding and subtracting rational expressions:

- Find least common denominator (LCD).

- Write each expression using the LCD.

- Add or subtract the numerators.

- Simplify as needed.

Examples:

Example 1. Solve. $\frac{4}{2x+3} + \frac{x-2}{2x+3} =$

Solution: The denominators are equal. Then, use fractions addition rule:

$$\frac{a}{c} \pm \frac{b}{c} = \frac{a \pm b}{c} \rightarrow \frac{4}{2x+3} + \frac{x-2}{2x+3} = \frac{4+(x-2)}{2x+3} = \frac{x+2}{2x+3}$$

Example 2. Solve. $\frac{x+4}{x-5} + \frac{x-4}{x+6} =$

Solution: Find the least common denominator of $(x-5)$ and $(x+6)$: $(x-5)(x+6)$

Then: $\frac{x+4}{x-5} + \frac{x-4}{x+6} = \frac{(x+4)(x+6)}{(x-5)(x+6)} + \frac{(x-4)(x-5)}{(x+6)(x-5)} = \frac{(x+4)(x+6)+(x-4)(x-5)}{(x+6)(x-5)}$

Expand: $(x+4)(x+6) + (x-4)(x-5) = 2x^2 + x + 44$

Then: $\frac{(x+4)(x+6)+(x-4)(x-5)}{(x+6)(x-5)} = \frac{2x^2+x+44}{(x+6)(x-5)} = \frac{2x^2+x+44}{x^2+x-30}$

Multiplying Rational Expressions

- Multiplying rational expressions is the same as multiplying fractions. First, multiply numerators and then multiply denominators. Then, simplify as needed.

Examples:

Example 1. Solve: $\frac{x+6}{x-1} \times \frac{x-1}{5} =$

Solution: Multiply numerators and denominators: $\frac{a}{b} \times \frac{c}{d} = \frac{a \times c}{b \times d}$

$$\frac{x+6}{x-1} \times \frac{x-1}{5} = \frac{(x+6)(x-1)}{5(x-1)}$$

Cancel the common factor: $(x-1)$

Then: $\frac{(x+6)(x-1)}{5(x-1)} = \frac{(x+6)}{5}$

Example 2. Solve: $\frac{x-2}{x+3} \times \frac{2x+6}{x-2} =$

Solution: Multiply numerators and denominators: $\frac{x-2}{x+3} \times \frac{2x+6}{x-2} = \frac{(x-2)(2x+6)}{(x+3)(x-2)}$

Cancel the common factor: $\frac{(x-2)(2x+6)}{(x+3)(x-2)} = \frac{(2x+6)}{(x+3)}$

Factor $2x+6 = 2(x+3)$

Then: $\frac{2(x+3)}{(x+3)} = 2$

bit.ly/3fclilU
Find more at

Dividing Rational Expressions

- To divide rational expressions, use the same method we use for dividing fractions. (Keep, Change, Flip)

- Keep the first rational expression, change the division sign to multiplication, and flip the numerator and denominator of the second rational expression. Then, multiply numerators and multiply denominators. Simplify as needed.

Examples:

Example 1. Solve. $\frac{x+2}{3x} \div \frac{x^2+5x+6}{3x^2+3x} =$

Solution: Use fractions division rule: $\frac{a}{b} \div \frac{c}{d} = \frac{a}{b} \times \frac{d}{c} = \frac{a \times d}{b \times c}$

$$\frac{x+2}{3x} \div \frac{x^2+5x+6}{3x^2+3x} = \frac{x+2}{3x} \times \frac{3x^2+3x}{x^2+5x+6} = \frac{(x+2)(3x^2+3x)}{(3x)(x^2+5x+6)}$$

Now, factorize the expressions $3x^2 + 3x$ and $(x^2 + 5x + 6)$. Then:

$3x^2 + 3x = 3x(x+1)$ and $x^2 + 5x + 6 = (x+2)(x+3)$

Simplify: $\frac{(x+2)(3x^2+3x)}{(3x)(x^2+5x+6)} = \frac{(x+2)(3x)(x+1)}{(3x)(x+2)(x+3)}$, cancel common factors. Then:

$$\frac{(x+2)(3x)(x+1)}{(3x)(x+2)(x+3)} = \frac{x+1}{x+3}$$

Example 2. Solve. $\frac{5x}{x+3} \div \frac{x}{2x+6} =$

Solution: Use fractions division rule: $\frac{a}{b} \div \frac{c}{d} = \frac{a}{b} \times \frac{d}{c} = \frac{a \times d}{b \times c}$

Then: $\frac{5x}{x+3} \div \frac{x}{2x+6} = \frac{5x}{x+3} \times \frac{2x+6}{x} = \frac{5x(2x+6)}{x(x+3)} = \frac{5x \times 2(x+3)}{x(x+3)}$

Cancel common factor: $\frac{5x \times 2(x+3)}{x(x+3)} = \frac{10x(x+3)}{x(x+3)} = 10$

Rational Equations

For solving rational equations, we can use following methods:

- **Converting to a common denominator:** In this method, you need to get a common denominator for both sides of the equation. Then, make numerators equal and solve for the variable.

- **Cross-multiplying:** This method is useful when there is only one fraction on each side of the equation. Simply multiply the first numerator by the second denominator and make the result equal to the product of the second numerator and the first denominator.

Examples:

Example 1. Solve. $\frac{x-2}{x+1} = \frac{x+4}{x-2}$

Solution: Use cross multiply method: if $\frac{a}{b} = \frac{c}{d}$, then: $a \times d = b \times c$

$\frac{x-2}{x+1} = \frac{x+4}{x-2} \rightarrow (x-2)(x-2) = (x+4)(x+1)$

Expand: $(x-2)^2 = x^2 - 4x + 4$ and $(x+4)(x+1) = x^2 + 5x + 4$,

Then: $x^2 - 4x + 4 = x^2 + 5x + 4$, Now, simplify: $x^2 - 4x = x^2 + 5x$, subtract both sides $(x^2 + 5x)$,

Then: $x^2 - 4x - (x^2 + 5x) = x^2 + 5x - (x^2 + 5x) \rightarrow -9x = 0 \rightarrow x = 0$

Example 2. Solve. $\frac{2x}{x-3} = \frac{2x+2}{2x-6}$

Solution: Multiply the numerator and denominator of the rational expression on the left by 2 to get a common denominator $(2x - 6)$. $\frac{2(2x)}{2(x-3)} = \frac{4x}{2x-6}$

Now, the denominators on both side of the equation are equal. Therefore, their numerators must be equal too.

$$\frac{4x}{2x-6} = \frac{2x+2}{2x-6} \rightarrow 4x = 2x + 2 \rightarrow 2x = 2 \rightarrow x = 1$$

Chapter 19: Practices

✏ **Simplify each expression.**

1) $\dfrac{\frac{2}{5}}{\frac{4}{7}} =$

2) $\dfrac{6}{\frac{5}{x}+\frac{2}{3x}} =$

3) $\dfrac{1-\frac{2}{x-1}}{1+\frac{4}{x+1}} =$

4) $\dfrac{x}{\frac{3}{4}-\frac{5}{x}} =$

✏ **Graph rational expressions.**

5) $f(x) = \dfrac{x^2}{5x+6}$

6) $f(x) = \dfrac{x^2+8x+10}{x+5}$

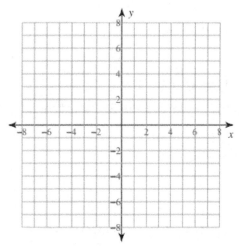
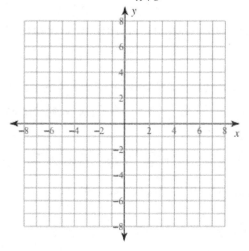

✏ **Simplify each expression.**

7) $\dfrac{5}{x+2} + \dfrac{x-1}{x+2} =$

8) $\dfrac{6}{x+5} - \dfrac{5}{x+5} =$

9) $\dfrac{7}{4x+10} + \dfrac{x-5}{4x+10} =$

✎ Simplify each expression.

10) $\dfrac{x+1}{x+5} \times \dfrac{x+6}{x+1} =$

11) $\dfrac{x+4}{x+9} \times \dfrac{x+9}{x+3} =$

12) $\dfrac{x+8}{x} \times \dfrac{2}{x+8} =$

13) $\dfrac{x+5}{x+1} \times \dfrac{x^2}{x+5} =$

14) $\dfrac{x-3}{x+2} \times \dfrac{2x+4}{x+4} =$

15) $\dfrac{x-6}{x+3} \times \dfrac{2x+6}{2x} =$

✎ Solve.

16) $\dfrac{5x}{4} \div \dfrac{5}{2} =$

17) $\dfrac{8}{3x} \div \dfrac{24}{x} =$

18) $\dfrac{3x}{x+4} \div \dfrac{x}{3x+12} =$

19) $\dfrac{2}{5x} \div \dfrac{16}{10x} =$

20) $\dfrac{36x}{5} \div \dfrac{4}{3} =$

21) $\dfrac{15x^2}{6} \div \dfrac{5x}{14} =$

✎ Solve each equation.

22) $\dfrac{1}{8x^2} = \dfrac{1}{4x^2} - \dfrac{1}{x} \rightarrow x = $ _____

23) $\dfrac{1}{x} + \dfrac{1}{9x} = \dfrac{5}{36} \rightarrow x = $ _____

24) $\dfrac{32}{2x^2} + 1 = \dfrac{8}{x} \rightarrow x = $ _____

25) $\dfrac{1}{x-5} = \dfrac{4}{x-5} + 1 \rightarrow x = $ _____

Effortless
Math
Education

Answers – Chapter 19

1) $\dfrac{7}{10}$

2) $\dfrac{18x}{17}$

3) $\dfrac{x^2-2x-3}{x^2+4x-5}$

4) $\dfrac{4x^2}{3x-20}$

5)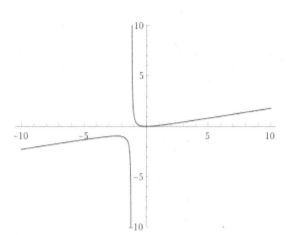

6)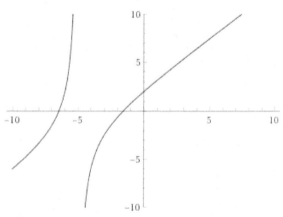

7) $\dfrac{x+4}{x+2}$

8) $\dfrac{1}{x+5}$

9) $\dfrac{x+2}{4x+10}$

10) $\dfrac{x+6}{x+5}$

11) $\dfrac{x+4}{x+3}$

12) $\dfrac{2}{x}$

13) $\dfrac{x^2}{x+1}$

14) $\dfrac{2(x-3)}{x+4}$

15) $\dfrac{x-6}{x}$

16) $\dfrac{x}{2}$

17) $\dfrac{1}{9}$

18) 9

19) $\dfrac{1}{4}$

20) $\dfrac{27x}{5}$

21) $7x$

22) $x=\dfrac{1}{8}$

23) $x=8$

24) $x=4$

25) $x=2$

20 Trigonometric Functions

Math topics that you'll learn in this Chapter:

- ☑ Angle and Angle Measure
- ☑ Trigonometric Functions
- ☑ Coterminal Angles and Reference Angles
- ☑ Evaluating Trigonometric Functions
- ☑ Missing Sides and Angles of a Right Triangle

185

Angle and Angle Measure

- To convert degrees to radians, use this formula:

$$\text{Radians} = \text{Degrees} \times \frac{\pi}{180}$$

- To convert radians to degrees, use this formula:

$$\text{Degrees} = \text{Radians} \times \frac{\pi}{180}$$

Examples:

Example 1. Convert 160 degrees to radian.

Solution: Use this formula: $\text{Radians} = \text{Degrees} \times \frac{\pi}{180}$

$\text{Radians} = 160 \times \frac{\pi}{180} = \frac{160\pi}{180} = \frac{8\pi}{9}$

Example 2. Convert radian measure $\frac{3\pi}{4}$ to degree measure.

Solution: Use this formula: $\text{Degrees} = \text{Radians} \times \frac{180}{\pi}$

$\text{Radians} = \frac{3\pi}{4} \times \frac{180}{\pi} = \frac{540\pi}{4\pi} = 135$

Example 3. Convert 150 degrees to radian.

Solution: Use this formula: $\text{Radians} = \text{Degrees} \times \frac{\pi}{180}$

$\text{Radians} = 150 \times \frac{\pi}{180} = \frac{150\pi}{180} = \frac{5\pi}{6}$

Example 4. Convert radian measure $\frac{3\pi}{4}$ to degree measure.

Solution: Use this formula: $\text{Degrees} = \text{Radians} \times \frac{180}{\pi}$

$\text{Radians} = \frac{2\pi}{3} \times \frac{180}{\pi} = \frac{360\pi}{3\pi} = 120$

Trigonometric Functions

- Trigonometric functions refer to the relation between the sides and angles of a right triangle. There are 6 trigonometric functions:

- Sine (sin), Cosine (cos), Tangent (tan), Secant (sec), Cosecant (csc), and Cotangent (cot)

- The three main trigonometric functions:

$$SOH - CAH - TOA, \ sin \ \theta = \frac{opposite}{hypotenuse}, \ Cos \ \theta = \frac{adjacent}{hypotenuse}, \ tan \ \theta = \frac{opposite}{adjacent}$$

- The reciprocal trigonometric functions:

$$csc \ x = \frac{1}{sin \ x}, \ sec \ x = \frac{1}{cos \ x}, \ cot \ \theta = \frac{1}{tan \ x}$$

- Learn common trigonometric functions:

θ	0°	30°	45°	60°	90°
$sin \ \theta$	0	$\frac{1}{2}$	$\frac{\sqrt{2}}{2}$	$\frac{\sqrt{3}}{2}$	1
$cos \ \theta$	1	$\frac{\sqrt{3}}{2}$	$\frac{\sqrt{2}}{2}$	$\frac{1}{2}$	0
$tan \ \theta$	0	$\frac{\sqrt{3}}{3}$	1	$\sqrt{3}$	Undefined

Examples:

Find each trigonometric function.

Example 1. $sin \ 120°$

Solution: Use the following property: $sin(x) = cos(90° - x)$
$sin \ 120° = cos(90° - 120°) = cos(-30°) = \frac{\sqrt{3}}{2}$

Example 2. $tan \ 120°$

Solution: Use the following property: $tan(x) = \frac{sin \ (x)}{cos(x)}$

$$tan(x) = \frac{sin(x)}{cos(x)} = tan(120) = \frac{sin(120)}{cos(120)} = \frac{\frac{\sqrt{3}}{2}}{-\frac{1}{2}} = -\sqrt{3}$$

Coterminal Angles and Reference Angles

- Coterminal angles are equal angles.

- To find a Coterminal of an angle, add or subtract 360 degrees (or 2π for radians) to the given angle.

- Reference angle is the smallest angle that you can make from the terminal side of an angle with the x-axis.

Examples:

Example 1. Find a positive and a negative Coterminal angle to angle $65°$.

Solution:

$65° - 360° = -295°$

$65° + 360° = 425°$

$-295°$ and a $425°$ are Coterminal with angle $65°$.

Example 2. Find positive and negative Coterminal angles to angle $\frac{\pi}{2}$.

Solution:

$\frac{\pi}{2} + 2\pi = \frac{5\pi}{2}$

$\frac{\pi}{2} - 2\pi = -\frac{3\pi}{2}$

Example 3. Find a positive and a negative Coterminal angle to angle $80°$.

Solution:

$80° - 360° = -280°$

$80° + 360° = 440°$

$-280°$ and a $440°$ are Coterminal with angle $80°$.

Evaluating Trigonometric Functions

- **Step 1:** Find the reference angle. (It is the smallest angle that you can make from the terminal side of an angle with the x-axis.)

- **Step 2:** Determine the quadrant of the function. Depending on the quadrant in which the function lies, the answer will be either positive or negative.

- **Step 3:** Find the trigonometric function of the reference angle.

Examples:

Example 1. Find the exact value of trigonometric function. $tan\ \frac{5\pi}{4}$

Solution: Rewrite the angle for $\frac{5\pi}{4}$:

$tan\ \frac{5\pi}{4} = tan\left(\frac{4\pi+\pi}{4}\right) = tan\left(\pi + \frac{1}{4}\pi\right)$

Use the periodicity of tan: $tan(x + \pi \cdot k) = tan(x)$

$tan\left(\pi + \frac{1}{4}\pi\right) = tan\left(\frac{1}{4}\pi\right) = 1$

Example 2. Find the exact value of trigonometric function. $cos\ 225°$

Solution: First, recall that $cos\ (225°)$ is in the third quadrant and cosine is negative in the third quadrant.

The reference angle of $225°$ is $45°$. Therefore, $cos\ 225° = -cos\ 45°$

$cos\ 45° = \frac{\sqrt{2}}{2}$. Then, $-cos\ 45° = -\frac{\sqrt{2}}{2}$

Example 3. Find the exact value of trigonometric function. $sin\ \frac{7\pi}{6}$

Solution: Rewrite the $sin\ \frac{7\pi}{6}$.

$sin\ \frac{7\pi}{6} = sin\left(\frac{\pi}{6} + \pi\right) = cos\left(\frac{\pi}{6}\right)$ (complementary arcs)

Trig Table of Special Arcs gives: $cos\ \frac{\pi}{6} = \frac{\sqrt{3}}{2}$

bit.ly/3aUyyQy

Find more at

Missing Sides and Angles of a Right Triangle

- By using three main trigonometric functions (Sine, Cosine or Tangent), we can find an unknown side in a right triangle when we have one length, and one angle (apart from the right angle).

- A right triangle with Adjacent and Opposite sides and Hypotenuse is shown below.

- Recall the three main trigonometric functions:

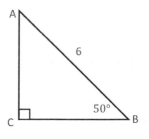

SOH – CAH – TOA, $sin\,\theta = \frac{opposite}{hypotenuse}$, $Cos\,\theta = \frac{adjacent}{hypotenuse}$, $tan\,\theta = \frac{opposite}{adjacent}$

- To find missing angles, use inverse of trigonometric functions (examples: $sin^{-1}, cos^{-1}, and\ tan^{-1}$)

Examples:

Example 1. Find side AC in the following triangle. Round your answer to the nearest tenth.

Solution: $sin\,\theta = \frac{opposite}{hypotenuse}$. $sine\ 50° = \frac{AC}{6} \rightarrow 6 \times sin\ 50° = AC$,

Now use a calculator to find $sine\ 50°$.

$$sin\ 50° \approx 0.766$$

$AC = 6 \times 0.766 = 4.596$, rounding to the nearest tenth: $4.596 \approx 4.6$

Example 2. Find the value of x in the following triangle.

Solution: $cos\,\theta = \frac{adjacent}{hypotenuse} \rightarrow cos\,x = \frac{10}{14} = \frac{5}{7}$

Use a calculator to find inverse cosine:

$$cos^{-1}\left(\frac{5}{7}\right) = 44.41° \approx 44°$$

Then: $x = 44$

Chapter 20: Practices

✎ Convert each degree measure into radians.

1) $135° =$

2) $80° =$

3) $270° =$

4) $92° =$

✎ Evaluate.

5) $\sin 90° =$ _____

6) $\sin -330° =$ _____

7) $\tan -30° =$ _____

8) $\cot \frac{2\pi}{3} =$ _____

9) $\tan \frac{\pi}{3} =$ _____

10) $\sin \frac{2\pi}{6} =$ _____

✎ Find a positive and a negative Coterminal angle for each angle.

11) $140° =$

   Positive = _____

   Negative = _____

12) $-165° =$

   Positive = _____

   Negative = _____

13) $190° =$

   Positive = _____

   Negative = _____

14) $\frac{5\pi}{4} =$

   Positive = _____

   Negative = _____

15) $\frac{2\pi}{9} =$

   Positive = _____

   Negative = _____

16) $-\frac{7\pi}{9} =$

   Positive = _____

   Negative = _____

Effortless Math Education

✎ **Find the exact value of each trigonometric function.**

17) $\cos 180° =$ _____

18) $\cos -270° =$ _____

19) $\tan 225° =$ _____

20) $\sin \frac{\pi}{4} =$ _____

21) $\csc 330° =$ _____

22) $\tan -120° =$ _____

✎ **Find the value of x in each triangle.**

23) _____

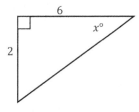

24) _____

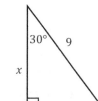

25) _____

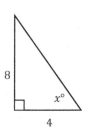

26) _____

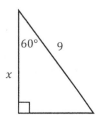

27) _____

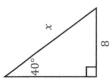

28)   _____

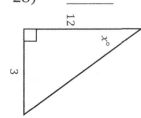

Effortless
Math
Education

Answers – Chapter 20

1) $\frac{3}{4}\pi$

2) $\frac{4}{9}\pi$

3) $\frac{3}{2}\pi$

4) $\frac{23}{45}\pi$

5) 1

6) $\frac{1}{2}$

7) $-\frac{\sqrt{3}}{3}$

8) $-\frac{\sqrt{3}}{3}$

9) $\sqrt{3}$

10) $\frac{\sqrt{3}}{2}$

11) Positive = $500°$, Negative = $-220°$

12) Positive = $195°$, Negative = $-525°$

13) Positive = $550°$, Negative = $-170°$

14) Positive = $\frac{13\pi}{4}$, Negative = $-\frac{3\pi}{4}$

15) Positive = $\frac{20\pi}{9}$, Negative = $-\frac{16\pi}{9}$

16) Positive = $\frac{11\pi}{9}$, Negative = $-\frac{25\pi}{9}$

17) -1

18) 0

19) 1

20) $\frac{\sqrt{2}}{2}$

21) -2

22) $\sqrt{3}$

23) 18

24) 7.8

25) 63

26) 4.5

27) 12.45

28) 14

Time to Test

Time to refine your skill with a practice examination

Take an ALEKS Mathematics practice test to simulate the test day experience. After you've finished, score your test using the answers and explanations section.

Before You Start

- ❖ You'll need a pencil and scratch papers to take the test.
- ❖ For these practice tests, don't time yourself. Spend time as much as you need.
- ❖ After you've finished the test, review the answer key to see where you went wrong.

Good luck!

ALEKS Mathematics Practice Test 1

2023

Total number of questions: 30

Total time (Calculator): No time limit

Calculators are permitted for ALEKS Math Test.

(On a real ALEKS test, there is an onscreen calculator to use.)

1) If $f(x) = 4x - 2$ and $g(x) = x^2 - x$, then find $\left(\frac{f}{g}\right)(x)$.

2) A bank is offering 4.5% simple interest on a savings account. If you deposit $12,000, how much interest will you earn in two years?

3) If the ratio of home fans to visiting fans in a crowd is $3:2$ and all 24,000 seats in a stadium are filled, how many visiting fans are in attendance?

4) If the interior angles of a quadrilateral are in the ratio $2:3:3:4$, what is the measure of the largest angle?

5) If the area of a circle is 49 square meters, what is its diameter?

6) The length of a rectangle is $\frac{5}{4}$ times its width. If the width is 20, what is the perimeter of this rectangle?

7) In the figure below, line A is parallel to line B. What is the value of angle x?

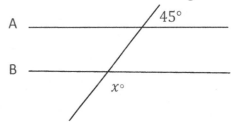

8) An angle is equal to one ninth of its supplement. What is the measure of that angle?

9) What is the value of y in the following system of equations?

$$2x + 5y = 11$$
$$4x - 2y = -14$$

10) Last week 25,000 fans attended a football match. This week three times as many bought tickets, but one sixth of them cancelled their tickets. How many are attending this week?

11) If $sin\ A = \frac{1}{3}$ in a right triangle and the angle A is an acute angle, then what is $cos\ A$?

12) In the standard (x, y) coordinate system plane, what is the area of the circle with the following equation?

$$(x + 2)^2 + (y - 4)^2 = 25$$

13) Convert 580,000 to scientific notation.

14) The ratio of boys to girls in a school is $2:3$. If there are 500 students in a school, how many boys are in the school.

15) If 150% of a number is 75, then what is 80% of that number?

16) If $A = \begin{bmatrix} -1 & 2 \\ 1 & -2 \end{bmatrix}$ and $B = \begin{bmatrix} 3 & 1 \\ -2 & 3 \end{bmatrix}$, then $2A - B =$

17) What is the solution of the following inequality?

$$|x - 2| \geq 4$$

18) If $\tan x = \frac{8}{15}$, then $\sin x = ?$

19) $(x^6)^{\frac{7}{8}}$ equal to?

20) What are the zeroes of the function $f(x) = x^3 + 5x^2 + 6x$?

21) If $x + sin^2a + cos^2a = 3$, then $x = ?$

22) If $\sqrt{5x} = \sqrt{y}$, then $x =$

23) The average weight of 18 girls in a class is $55\ kg$ and the average weight of 32 boys in the same class is $62\ kg$. What is the average weight of all the 50 students in that class?

24) What is the value of the expression $5(x - 2y) + (2 - x)^2$ when $x = 3$ and

$y = -3$?

25) Sophia purchased a sofa for $530.40. The sofa is regularly priced at $631. What was the percent discount Sophia received on the sofa?

26) If one angle of a right triangle measures 60°, what is the sine of the other acute angle?

27) Simplify $\frac{4-3i}{-4i}$?

28) The average of five consecutive numbers is 40. What is the smallest number?

29) What is the slope of a line that is perpendicular to the line

$$4x - 2y = 14?$$

30) If $f(x)=2x^3+ 4$ and $g(x)=\frac{1}{x}$, what is the value of $f(g(x))$?

This is the end of Practice Test 1.

ALEKS Mathematics Practice Test 2

2023

Total number of questions: 30

Total time (Calculator): No time limit

Calculators are permitted for ALEKS Math Test.

(On a real ALEKS test, there is an onscreen calculator to use.)

1) How many tiles of $8 \ cm^2$ is needed to cover a floor of dimension $6 \ cm$ by $24 \ cm$?

2) What is the area of a square whose diagonal is $8 \ cm$?

3) What is the value of x in the following figure?

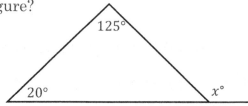

4) What is the value of y in the following system of equation?

$$3x - 4y = -20$$
$$-x + 2y = 10$$

5) How long does a 420–miles trip take moving at 50 miles per hour (mph)?

6) When 40% of 60 is added to 12% of 600, the resulting number is:

7) What is the solution of the following inequality?

$$|x - 10| \leq 3$$

8) In the following figure, ABCD is a rectangle, and E and F are points on AD and DC, respectively. The area of $\triangle BED$ is 16, and the area of $\triangle BDF$ is 18. What is the perimeter of the rectangle?

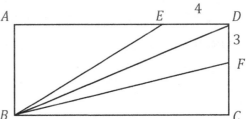

9) If a tree casts a 24–foot shadow at the same time that a 3 feet yardstick casts a 2–foot shadow, what is the height of the tree?

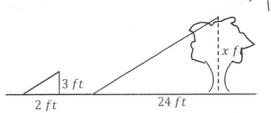

10) A ladder leans against a wall forming a 60° angle between the ground and the ladder. If the bottom of the ladder is 30 feet away from the wall, how long is the ladder?

11) Simplify. $2x^2 + 3y^5 - x^2 + 2z^3 - 2y^2 + 2x^3 - 2y^5 + 5z^3$

12) In five successive hours, a car traveled $40\ km, 45\ km, 50\ km, 35\ km$ and $55\ km$. In the next five hours, it traveled with an average speed of $50\ km\ per\ hour$. Find the total distance the car traveled in 10 hours.

13) In the following figure, ABCD is a rectangle. If $a = \sqrt{3}$, and $b = 2a$, find the area of the shaded region. (the shaded region is a trapezoid)

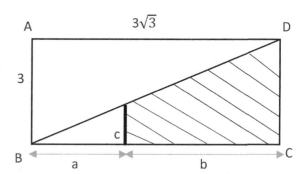

14) 6 liters of water are poured into an aquarium that's $15cm$ long, $5cm$ wide, and $90cm$ high. How many centimeters will the water level in the aquarium rise due to this added water? ($1\ liter\ of\ water = 1,000\ cm^3$)

15) If a box contains red and blue balls in ratio of $2:3$, how many red balls are there if 90 blue balls are in the box?

16) A chemical solution contains 4% alcohol. If there is $24\ ml$ of alcohol, what is the volume of the solution?

17) If $\frac{3x}{16} = \frac{x-1}{4}$, $x =$

18) Simplify $(-5 + 9i)(3 + 5i)$.

19) If θ is an acute angle and $sin\ \theta = \frac{4}{5}$ then $cos\ \theta =$

20) If 60% of x equal to 30% of 20, then what is the value of $(x + 5)^2$?

21) A boat sails 40 miles south and then 30 miles east. How far is the boat from its start point?

22) What is the value of x in the following equation? $log_4(x+2) - log_4(x-2) = 1$

23) A number is chosen at random from 1 to 25. Find the probability of not selecting a composite number.

24) Find AC in the following triangle. Round your answer to the nearest tenth.

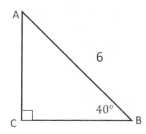

25) If $y = 4ab + 3b^3$, what is y when $a = 2$ and $b = 3$?

26) If $f(x) = 5 + x$ and $g(x) = -x^2 - 1 - 2x$, then find $(g - f)(x)$.

27) If cotangent of an angel β is 1, then the tangent of angle β is …

28) When point $A\,(10, 3)$ is reflected over the y −axis to get the point B, what are the coordinates of point B?

29) What is the average of circumference of figure A and area of figure B? $(\pi = 3)$

Figure A Figure B

30) If $f(x) = 2x^3 + 5x^2 + 2x$ and $g(x) = -2$, what is the value of $f(g(x))$?

This is the end of Practice Test 2.

ALEKS Mathematics
Practice Tests
Answers and Explanations

ALEKS Mathematics Practice Test 1 Answers and Explanations

1) **The answer is** $\frac{4x-2}{x^2-x}$

$$\left(\frac{f}{g}\right)(x) = \frac{f(x)}{g(x)} = \frac{4x-2}{x^2-x}$$

2) **The answer is** $1,080$

Use simple interest formula: $I = prt$ (I = interest, p = principal, r = rate, t = time), $I = (12,000)(0.045)(2) = 1,080$

3) **The answer is** $9,600$

Number of visiting fans: $\frac{2 \times 24,000}{5} = 9,600$

4) **The answer is** $120°$

The sum of all angles in a quadrilateral is 360 degrees. Let x be the smallest angle in the quadrilateral. Then the angles are: $2x, 3x, 3x, 4x$, $2x + 3x + 3x + 4x = 360 \rightarrow 12x = 360 \rightarrow x = 30$, The angles in the quadrilateral are: $60°, 90°, 90°,$ and $120°$

5) **The answer is** $\frac{14\sqrt{\pi}}{\pi}$

Formula for the area of a circle is: $A = \pi r^2$, Using 49 for the area of the circle we have: $49 = \pi r^2$, Let's solve for the radius (r).

$$\frac{49}{\pi} = r^2 \rightarrow r = \sqrt{\frac{49}{\pi}} = \frac{7}{\sqrt{\pi}} = \frac{7}{\sqrt{\pi}} \times \frac{\sqrt{\pi}}{\sqrt{\pi}} = \frac{7\sqrt{\pi}}{\pi}$$

Then, the diameter of the circle is: $d = 2r \rightarrow d = 2 \times \frac{7\sqrt{\pi}}{\pi} = \frac{14\sqrt{\pi}}{\pi}$

6) **The answer is** 90

Length of the rectangle is: $\frac{5}{4} \times 20 = 25$, perimeter of rectangle is: $2 \times (20 + 25) = 90$

7) The answer is 135°

The angle x and 45 are complementary angles. Therefore: $x + 45 = 180 \rightarrow x = 180° - 45° = 135°$

8) The answer is 18

The sum of supplement angles is 180. Let x be that angle. Therefore, $x + 9x = 180$
$10x = 180$, divide both sides by 10: $x = 18$

9) The answer is 3

Solving Systems of Equations by Elimination: Multiply the first equation by (-2), then add it to the second equation.
$$-2(2x + 5y = 11) \atop 4x - 2y = -14 \Rightarrow {-4x - 10y = -22 \atop 4x - 2y = -14} \Rightarrow -12y = -36 \Rightarrow y = 3$$

10) The answer is 62,500

Three times of 25,000 is 75,000. One sixth of them cancelled their tickets. One sixth of 75,000 equals 12,500 ($\frac{1}{6} \times 72,000 = 12,500$). 62,500 ($72,000 - 12,000 = 62,500$) fans are attending this week.

11) The answer is $\frac{\sqrt{8}}{3}$

$sinA = \frac{1}{3} \Rightarrow$ Since $sin\theta = \frac{opposite}{hypotenuse}$, we have the following right triangle. Then:
$c = \sqrt{3^2 - 1^2} = \sqrt{9 - 1} = \sqrt{8}, cosA = \frac{\sqrt{8}}{3}$

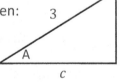

12) The answer is 25π

The equation of a circle in standard form is: $(x - h)^2 + (y - k)^2 = r^2$, where r is the radius of the circle. In this circle the radius is 5. $r^2 = 25 \rightarrow r = 5$, $(x + 2)^2 + (y - 4)^2 = 25$
Area of a circle: $A = \pi r^2 = \pi(5)^2 = 25\pi$

13) The answer is 5.8×10^5

$580,000 = 5.8 \times 10^5$

14) The answer is 200

The ratio of boy to girls is $2:3$. Therefore, there are 2 boys out of 5 students. To find the answer, first divide the total number of students by 5, then multiply the result by 2.

$500 \div 5 = 100 \Rightarrow 100 \times 2 = 200$

15) The answer is 40

First, find the number. Let x be the number. Write the equation and solve for x.

150% of a number is 75, then: $1.5 \times x = 75 \Rightarrow x = 75 \div 1.5 = 50$

80% of 50 is: $0.8 \times 50 = 40$

16) The answer is $\begin{bmatrix} -5 & 3 \\ 4 & -7 \end{bmatrix}$

First, find $2A$. $A = \begin{bmatrix} -1 & 2 \\ 1 & -2 \end{bmatrix}$; $2A = 2 \times \begin{bmatrix} -1 & 2 \\ 1 & -2 \end{bmatrix} = \begin{bmatrix} -2 & 4 \\ 2 & -4 \end{bmatrix}$, Now, solve for

$2A - B. 2A - B = \begin{bmatrix} -2 & 4 \\ 2 & -4 \end{bmatrix} - \begin{bmatrix} 3 & 1 \\ -2 & 3 \end{bmatrix} = \begin{bmatrix} -2-3 & 4-1 \\ 2-(-2) & -4-3 \end{bmatrix} = \begin{bmatrix} -5 & 3 \\ 4 & -7 \end{bmatrix}$

17) The answer is $x \geq 6 \cup x \leq -2$

$x - 2 \geq 4 \rightarrow x \geq 4 + 2 \rightarrow x \geq 6$, Or $x - 2 \leq -4 \rightarrow x \leq -4 + 2 \rightarrow x \leq -2$

Then, solution is: $x \geq 6 \cup x \leq -2$

18) The answer is $\frac{8}{17}$

$\tan = \frac{opposite}{adjacent}$, and $\tan x = \frac{8}{15}$, therefore, the opposite side of the angle x is 8 and the adjacent side is 15. Let's draw the triangle.

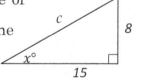

Using Pythagorean theorem, we have:

$a^2 + b^2 = c^2 \rightarrow 8^2 + 15^2 = c^2 \rightarrow 64 + 225 = c^2 \rightarrow c = 17$, $\sin x = \frac{opposite}{hypotenuse} = \frac{8}{17}$

19) The answer is $x^{\frac{21}{4}}$

$(x^6)^{\frac{7}{8}} = x^{6 \times \frac{7}{8}} = x^{\frac{42}{8}} = x^{\frac{21}{4}}$

20) The answer are $0, -2, -3$

Frist factor the function: $f(x) = x^3 + 5x^2 + 6x = x(x+2)(x+3)$, To find the zeros, $f(x)$ should be zero. $f(x) = x(x+2)(x+3) = 0$, Therefore, the zeros are: $x = 0$, $(x+2) = 0 \Rightarrow x = -2$, $(x+3) = 0 \Rightarrow x = -3$

21) The answer is 2

$sin^2 a + cos^2 a = 1$, then: $x + 1 = 3$, $x = 2$

22) The answer is $\frac{y}{5}$

Solve for x. $\sqrt{5x} = \sqrt{y}$. Square both sides of the equation: $(\sqrt{5x})^2 = (\sqrt{y})^2$; $5x = y$; $x = \frac{y}{5}$

23) The answer is 59.48

$average = \frac{sum\ of\ terms}{number\ of\ terms}$, The sum of the weight of all girls is:

$18 \times 55 = 990\ kg$

The sum of the weight of all boys is: $32 \times 62 = 1,984\ kg$, The sum of the weight of all students is: $990 + 1,984 = 2,974\ kg$. $average = \frac{2,974}{50} = 59.48$

24) The answer is 46

Plug in the value of x and y. $x = 3$ and $y = -3$

$5(x - 2y) + (2 - x)^2 = 5(3 - 2(-3)) + (2 - 3)^2 = 5(3 + 6) + (-1)^2 = 45 + 1 = 46$

25) The answer is 16%

The question is this: 530.40 is what percent of 631? Use percent formula: $part = \frac{percent}{100} \times whole$. $530.40 = \frac{percent}{100} \times 631 \Rightarrow 530.40 = \frac{percent \times 631}{100} \Rightarrow 53,040 = percent \times 631 \Rightarrow percent = \frac{53,040}{631} = 84$. 530.40 is 84% of 631. Therefore, the discount is: $100\% - 84\% = 16\%$

26) The answer is $\frac{1}{2}$

The relationship among all sides of right triangle $30° - 60° - 90°$ is provided in the following triangle: Sine of $30°$ equals to:
$\frac{opposite}{hypotenuse} = \frac{x}{2x} = \frac{1}{2}$

27) The answer is $\frac{3}{4} + i$

To simplify the fraction, multiply both numerator and denominator by i.

$\frac{4-3i}{-4i} \times \frac{i}{i} = \frac{4i-3i^2}{-4i^2}$, $i^2 = -1$, Then: $\frac{4i-3i^2}{-4i^2} = \frac{4i-3(-1)}{-4(-1)} = \frac{4i+3}{4} = \frac{4i}{4} + \frac{3}{4} = \frac{3}{4} + i$

28) The answer is 38

Let x be the smallest number. Then, these are the numbers: x, $x + 1$, $x + 2$, $x + 3$, $x + 4$

$average = \frac{sum\ of\ terms}{number\ of\ terms} \Rightarrow 40 = \frac{x+(x+1)+(x+2)+(x+3)+(x+4)}{5} \Rightarrow 40 = \frac{5x+10}{5} \Rightarrow$

$200 = 5x + 10 \Rightarrow 190 = 5x \Rightarrow x = 38$

29) The answer is $-\frac{1}{2}$

The equation of a line in slope intercept form is: $y = mx + b$, Solve for y. $4x - 2y = 14 \Rightarrow -2y = 14 - 4x \Rightarrow y = (14 - 4x) \div (-2) \Rightarrow y = 2x - 7$, The slope is 2. The slope of the line perpendicular to this line is:

$m_1 \times m_2 = -1 \Rightarrow 2 \times m_2 = -1 \Rightarrow m_2 = -\frac{1}{2}$

30) The answer is $\frac{2}{x^3} + 4$

$f\big(g(x)\big) = 2 \times (\frac{1}{x})^3 + 4 = \frac{2}{x^3} + 4$

ALEKS Mathematics Practice Test 2
Answers and Explanations

1) The answer is 18

The area of the floor is: $6\ cm \times 24\ cm = 144\ cm^2$.
The number is tiles needed $= 144 \div 8 = 18$

2) The answer is 32

The diagonal of the square is 8. Let x be the side.
Use Pythagorean Theorem: $a^2 + b^2 = c^2$
$x^2 + x^2 = 8^2 \Rightarrow 2x^2 = 8^2 \Rightarrow 2x^2 = 64 \Rightarrow x^2 = 32$
$$\Rightarrow x = \sqrt{32}$$
The area of the square is: $\sqrt{32} \times \sqrt{32} = 32$

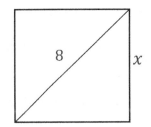

3) The answer is 145

$x = 20 + 125 = 145$

4) The answer is 5

Solve the system of equations by elimination method.
$\begin{array}{l} 3x - 4y = -20 \\ \underline{-x + 2y = 10} \end{array}$ Multiply the second equation by 3, then add it to the first

equation.

$\begin{array}{l} 3x - 4y = -20 \\ \underline{3(-x + 2y = 10)} \end{array} \Rightarrow \begin{array}{l} 3x - 4y = -20 \\ \underline{-3x + 6y = 30)} \end{array} \Rightarrow$ add the equations $2y = 10 \Rightarrow y = 5$

5) The answer is 8.4 hours

Use distance formula: $Distance = Rate \times time \Rightarrow 420 = 50 \times T$, divide both
sides by
50. $420 \div 50 = T \Rightarrow T = 8.4\ hours$. Change hours to minutes for the decimal
part. $0.4\ hours = 0.4 \times 60 = 24\ minutes$.

6) **The answer is 96**

40% of 60 equals to: $0.40 \times 60 = 24$, 12% of 600 equals to: $0.12 \times 600 = 72$
40% of 60 is added to 12% of 600: $24 + 72 = 96$

7) **The answer is $7 \leq x \leq 13$**

$|x - 10| \leq 3 \rightarrow -3 \leq x - 10 \leq 3 \rightarrow -3 + 10 \leq x - 10 + 10 \leq 3 + 10 \rightarrow 7 \leq x \leq 13$

8) **The answer is 40**

The area of ΔBED is 16, then: $\frac{4 \times AB}{2} = 16 \rightarrow 4 \times AB = 32 \rightarrow AB = 8$
The area of ΔBDF is 18, then: $\frac{3 \times BC}{2} = 18 \rightarrow 3 \times BC = 36 \rightarrow BC = 12$
The perimeter of the rectangle is $= 2 \times (8 + 12) = 40$

9) **The answer is 36 ft**

Write a proportion and solve for x. $\frac{3}{2} = \frac{x}{24} \Rightarrow 2x = 3 \times 24 \Rightarrow x = 36 \, ft$

10) **The answer is 60 ft**

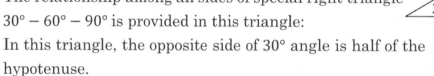

The relationship among all sides of special right triangle
$30° - 60° - 90°$ is provided in this triangle:
In this triangle, the opposite side of $30°$ angle is half of the
hypotenuse.
Draw the shape of this question:
The ladder is the hypotenuse. Therefore, the ladder is 60 ft.

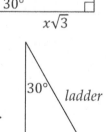

11) **The answer is $y^5 + 2x^3 + 7z^3 + x^2 - 2y^2$**

$2x^2 + 3y^5 - x^2 + 2z^3 - 2y^2 + 2x^3 - 2y^5 + 5z^3$
$$= 2x^2 - x^2 + 2x^3 - 2y^2 + 3y^5 - 2y^5 + 2z^3 + 5z^3$$
$$= x^2 + 2x^3 - 2y^2 + y^5 + 7z^3$$
Write the expression in standard form:
$x^2 + 2x^3 - 2y^2 + y^5 + 7z^3 = y^5 + 2x^3 + 7z^3 + x^2 - 2y^2$

12) The answer is 475

Add the first 5 numbers. $40 + 45 + 50 + 35 + 55 = 225$

To find the distance traveled in the next 5 hours, multiply the average by number of hours.

$Distance = Average \times Rate = 50 \times 5 = 250$. Add both numbers.

$250 + 225 = 475$

13) The answer is $4\sqrt{3}$

Based on triangle similarity theorem: $\frac{a}{a+b} = \frac{c}{3} \rightarrow c = \frac{3a}{a+b} = \frac{3\sqrt{3}}{3\sqrt{3}} = 1 \rightarrow$ area of shaded region is: $\left(\frac{c+3}{2}\right)(b) = \frac{4}{2} \times 2\sqrt{3} = 4\sqrt{3}$

14) The answer is $80 cm$

$One\ liter = 1,000\ cm^3 \rightarrow 6\ liters = 6,000\ cm^3;$

$6,000 = 15 \times 5 \times h \rightarrow h = \frac{6,000}{75} = 80 cm$

15) The answer is 60

$\frac{2}{3} \times 90 = 60$

16) The answer is $600\ ml$

4% of the volume of the solution is alcohol. Let x be the volume of the solution.

Then: $4\%\ of\ x = 24\ ml \Rightarrow 0.04\ x = 24 \Rightarrow x = 24 \div 0.04 = 600$

17) The answer is 4

Solve for x. $\frac{3x}{16} = \frac{x-1}{4}$. Multiply the second fraction by 4. $\frac{3x}{16} = \frac{4(x-1)}{4\times4}$. Tow denominators are equal. Therefore, the numerators must be equal. $3x = 4x - 4,\ 0 = x - 4\ ,4 = x$

18) The answer is $-60 + 2i$

We know that: $i = \sqrt{-1} \Rightarrow i^2 = -1$

$(-5 + 9i)(3 + 5i) = -15 - 25i + 27i + 45i^2 = -15 + 2i - 45 = -60 + 2i$

19) The answer is $\frac{3}{5}$

$sin\theta = \frac{4}{5} \Rightarrow$ we have following triangle, then

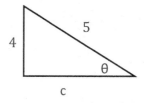

$c = \sqrt{5^2 - 4^2} = \sqrt{25 - 16} = \sqrt{9} = 3, cos\theta = \frac{3}{5}$

20) The answer is 225

$0.6x = (0.3) \times 20 \rightarrow x = 10 \rightarrow (x + 5)^2 = (15)^2 = 225$

21) The answer is 50 $miles$

Use the information provided in the question to draw the shape.
Use Pythagorean Theorem: $a^2 + b^2 = c^2$
$40^2 + 30^2 = c^2 \Rightarrow 1,600 + 900 = c^2 \Rightarrow 2,500 = c^2$
$\Rightarrow c = 50$

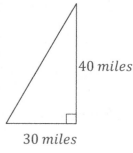

22) The answer is $\frac{10}{3}$

METHOD ONE
$log_4(x + 2) - log_4(x - 2) = 1$, Add $log_4(x - 2)$ to both sides
$log_4(x + 2) - log_4(x - 2) + log_4(x - 2) = 1 + log_4(x - 2)$
$log_4(x + 2) = 1 + log_4(x - 2)$
Apply logarithm rule: $a = log_b(b^a) \Rightarrow 1 = log_4(4^1) = log_4(4)$
then: $log_4(x + 2) = log_4(4) + log_4(x - 2)$
Logarithm rule: $log_c(a) + log_c(b) = log_c(ab)$
then: $log_4(4) + log_4(x - 2) = log_4(4(x - 2))$
$log_4(x + 2) = log_4(4(x - 2))$
When the logs have the same base: $log_b(f(x)) = log_b(g(x)) = f(x) = g(x)$
$(x + 2) = 4(x - 2)$, $x = \frac{10}{3}$
METHOD TWO
We know that: $log_a b - log_a c = log_a\frac{b}{c}$ and $log_a b = c \Rightarrow b = a^c$
Then: $log_4(x + 2) - log_4(x - 2) = log_4\frac{x+2}{x-2} = 1 \Rightarrow \frac{x+2}{x-2} = 4^1 = 4 \Rightarrow x + 2 = 4(x - 2)$
$\Rightarrow x + 2 = 4x - 8 \Rightarrow 4x - x = 8 + 2 \rightarrow 3x = 10 \Rightarrow x = \frac{10}{3}$

23) The answer is $\frac{2}{5}$

Set of number that are not composite between 1 and 25:

$A = \{1, 2, 3, 5, 7, 11, 13, 17, 19, 23\}$

$Probability = \dfrac{number\ of\ desired\ outcomes}{number\ of\ total\ outcomes} = \dfrac{10}{25} = \dfrac{2}{5}$

24) The answer is 3.9

$sine\ \theta = \dfrac{opposite}{hypotenuse}.\ sine\ 40° = \dfrac{AC}{6} \rightarrow 6 \times sine\ 40° = AC,$

Now use a calculator to find $sine\ 40°$. $sine\ 40° \cong 0.642 \rightarrow AC \cong 3.9$

25) The answer is 105

$y = 4ab + 3b^3$. Plug in the values of a and b in the equation: $a = 2$ and $b = 3$

$y = 4(2)(3) + 3\ (3)^3 = 24 + 3(27) = 24 + 81 = 105$

26) The answer is $-x^2 - 3x - 6$

$(g - f)(x) = g(x) - f(x) = (-x^2 - 1 - 2x) - (5 + x)$

$-x^2 - 1 - 2x - 5 - x = -x^2 - 3x - 6$

27) The answer is 1

$tangent\ \beta = \dfrac{1}{cotangent\ \beta} = \dfrac{1}{1} = 1$

28) The answer is $(-10, 3)$

When points are reflected over y-axis, the value of y in the coordinates doesn't change and the sign of x changes. Therefore, the coordinates of point B is $(-10, 3)$.

29) The answer is 60

Perimeter of figure A is: $2\pi r = 2\pi \dfrac{20}{2} = 20\pi = 20 \times 3 = 60$

Area of figure B is: $5 \times 12 = 60$, $Average = \dfrac{60 + 60}{2} = \dfrac{120}{2} = 60$

30) The answer is 0

$g(x) = -2$, then $f\big(g(x)\big) = f(-2) = 2\ (-2)^3 + 5(-2)^2 + 2(-2) = -16 + 20 - 4 = 0$

Receive the PDF version of this book or get another FREE book!

Thank you for using our Book!

Do you LOVE this book?

Then, you can get the PDF version of this book or another book absolutely FREE!

Please email us at:

info@EffortlessMath.com

for details.

Author's Final Note

I hope you enjoyed reading this book. You've made it through the book! Great job!

First of all, thank you for purchasing this study guide. I know you could have picked any number of books to help you prepare for your ALEKS Math test, but you picked this book and for that I am extremely grateful.

It took me years to write this study guide for the ALEKS Math because I wanted to prepare a comprehensive ALEKS Math study guide to help test takers make the most effective use of their valuable time while preparing for the test.

After teaching and tutoring math courses for over a decade, I've gathered my personal notes and lessons to develop this study guide. It is my greatest hope that the lessons in this book could help you prepare for your test successfully.

If you have any questions, please contact me at reza@effortlessmath.com and I will be glad to assist. Your feedback will help me to greatly improve the quality of my books in the future and make this book even better. Furthermore, I expect that I have made a few minor errors somewhere in this study guide. If you think this to be the case, please let me know so I can fix the issue as soon as possible.

If you enjoyed this book and found some benefit in reading this, I'd like to hear from you and hope that you could take a quick minute to post a review on the book's Amazon page.

I personally go over every single review, to make sure my books really are reaching out and helping students and test takers. Please help me help ALEKS Math test takers, by leaving a review!

I wish you all the best in your future success!

Reza Nazari

Math teacher and author

Made in the USA
Coppell, TX
26 November 2024

41066580R00131